STARGAZERS:
STORIES OF THE FIRST PHILOSOPHERS

STARGAZERS:

STORIES OF THE FIRST PHILOSOPHERS

Paul Rossetti Bjarnason

BOOKS

Winchester, U.K.
New York, U.S.A.

First published by O Books, 2007
O Books is an imprint of John Hunt Publishing Ltd.,
The Bothy, Deershot Lodge, Park Lane, Ropley, Hants, SO24 0BE, UK
office1@o-books.net
www.o-books.net

Distribution in:

UK and Europe
Orca Book Services
orders@orcabookservices.co.uk
Tel: 01202 665432
Fax: 01202 666219 Int. code (44)

USA and Canada
NBN
custserv@nbnbooks.com
Tel: 1 800 462 6420
Fax: 1 800 338 4550

Australia and New Zealand
Brumby Books
sales@brumbybooks.com.au

Tel: 61 3 9761 5535
Fax: 61 3 9761 7095

Far East (offices in Singapore, Thailand,
Hong Kong, Taiwan)
Pansing Distribution Pte Ltd
kemal@pansing.com
Tel: 65 6319 9939
Fax: 65 6462 5761

South Africa
Alternative Books
altbook@peterhyde.co.za
Tel: 021 447 5300
Fax: 021 447 1430

Text copyright Paul Bjarnason 2007

Design: Stuart Davies

ISBN: 978 1 84694 058 3

A CIP catalogue record for this book is available from the British Library.

Printed in the US by Maple Vail

Cover photo: Parthenon by Palma Bjarnason

DEDICATION

To Valerie, who helped so much along the way;
to Palma, who inspired this book;
to Rosa, who loves to know *why*;
anche a mia madre, Palma Rosa Rossetti,
una luce di bontà nella mia vita.

CONTENTS

PREFACE

This book has its origin in a question asked of me more than a dozen years ago by my daughter: *What is philosophy?* Our brief discussion of the subject ended with my promise to write a little book for her. After thinking for a while, I decided to trace philosophy to its beginnings, depicting the ancient philosophers – the ones who invented philosophy – in the very act of *being philosophers*. This, I reasoned, might be an ideal way of showing what philosophy is.

As it turned out, I wrote the first six or seven chapters within a short time, but then was sidetracked by other responsibilities. Eventually, many years later, I was able to get back to work and to honour my promise. The result is *Stargazers: Stories of the first philosophers*, a book for everyone who wants to know something about philosophy, or, at least, about what it was in the beginning.

Stargazers consists of twenty-one stories which take the reader on a journey from the Babylonian New Year Festival in about 1400 BC to Rome in AD 265, and – an equally great distance intellectually – from the myth of Marduk, king of the gods, to the rational mysticism of Plotinus the Neoplatonist. The philosophers act and speak for themselves as we watch and listen; and the reader is invited to become critic, a task which requires yet more reading and thinking. If to these are wedded a conscious choice of a way of living in the world and a rational discourse to examine and justify that choice, then the reader will have gone beyond critic to philosopher.

Each of the twenty-one chapters begins with a prelude providing a context for the story that follows it. In addition, there is a prologue outlining the book and an epilogue drawing some conclusions. There are also several helpful guides for the reader: a map giving meaning to the Greek and Roman place-names mentioned throughout the book; a chronology of the period covered in the text; a notes section clarifying a few essential points, as well as providing bibliographic information; and a select list of further reading. Philosophical terms are defined in context. It is hoped that these aids will help to make the reading of *Stargazers* an experience both pleasant and rewarding.

In some places in the text the personal pronoun *he* is used in place of the more cumbersome equivalent "he or she"; it is to be understood also that wherever *man* is used in a general sense, the meaning "men and women" is intended. Such usage reflects a traditional English language bias in favour of the male, but it does not reflect any such prejudice on the author's part.

✳

I would like to express my sincere gratitude to the following people for their assistance and encouragement at various times during work on this book: Thomas Petersen, Gordon Whitney, and the late William J. Davison, close friends and colleagues, and my son-in-law, Dimitrios Kontogiannis, all of whom read and offered helpful comments on portions of the manuscript; my daughter, Palma, whose impeccable sense of style helped render many passages more elegant than they would otherwise have been; and especially my wife, Valerie, whose close reading and editorial skill enabled me to improve the flow and consistency of the whole text.

I would like to thank also those others who took time to read all or part of the manuscript and to provide valuable observations: Professor Philip Allingham, Professor Dane Gordon, Dr. Geoffrey Klempner, Mr. Andrew Sewell, and Professor Eiichi Shimomisse, all of whose positive comments served to strengthen my conviction that *Stargazers* is a book for everyone.

Finally, three names must be mentioned *in memoriam*. Each was a true philosopher, self-taught and profoundly learned in a unique way: Douglas Ivan Hepburn – mentor, friend, Eastern mystic, and at one time world's strongest man; E.D. (Doug) Barton, my wife's uncle, who was a mystic and whose copy of Plotinus' *Enneads*, complete with handwritten notations, I have had the privilege of reading; and Harry "Tiny" Davis, a gentle giant and modern Diogenes, who read widely, lived simply, and walked to the *agora* every day, exchanging opinions on any subject with whomever he met, giving to others everything good that came his way. To these I am grateful for their having provided me with living examples of that ancient way of life known as *philosophia*, the love of wisdom.

Paul Rossetti Bjarnason
Vancouver, Canada
February, 2007

PROLOGUE

Had we never seen the stars, and the sun, and the heaven, none of the words which we have spoken would ever have been uttered. But now the sight of day and night, and the months and the revolutions of the years, have created number, and have given us a conception of time, and the power of inquiring about the nature of the universe. And from this source we have derived philosophy, than which no greater good ever was or will be given by the gods to mortal man.

PLATO

Stargazers is the story of the first philosophers of the western world, a story as much about their lives as about their ideas, for ancient philosophy on the whole was as much a choice of a way of life as it was a willingness to justify that choice through the use of human reason. Socrates is a perfect example of this duality: the life he chose for himself – or, as he put it, that was chosen for him by the Delphic god and by his personal *daimon*, or spiritual guide – was different from that of other men; and so was the discourse he used to justify both his way of living and his constant questioning of himself and others, in search of truth and on behalf of virtue.

Yet any attempt to tell the story of the ancient philosophers is beset by difficulties. In the first place, many of the earliest philosophers wrote nothing, expounding their ideas instead in public to whoever was willing to listen. Pythagoras, one of history's most influential thinkers, was among these.

Secondly, the works of those who did write were often lost to future generations, forcing scholars to rely on reports of others about their writings. This is especially true of the Presocratic philosophers – those who preceded Socrates – all of whose "fragments" of major works have been found in the writings of others. Such scanty evidence is bound to lead to inconclusiveness. Thus, many of these fragments are open to widely varying interpretations and have therefore been given a number of possible meanings.

Finally, it is clear that the "doxographers," or chroniclers of the beliefs of the early philosophers, sometimes exaggerated their accounts or received them at so great a distance from the original that it is impossible to ascertain their true value. This difficulty is compounded by the fact that in some instances there is either a lack of any supporting evidence whatsoever or else there are conflicting reports. In spite of such limitations, however, there is a substantial tradition surrounding the lives of the first philosophers, including a plethora of anecdotes which, though of doubtful status, are nonetheless worth including in any story of the philosophers, for they are both fascinating and memorable.

On First Philosophy

Philosophy gave to the world the first rational explanations of the origin and nature of the cosmos and of man's place therein. In doing so, it opposed itself to mythical accounts that referred all things to the various gods who ultimately controlled them. In such a context, the importance of Thales' assertion that everything comes from and is reducible to water lay in its radical status as an essentially *rational* account. The idea of explaining the diversity of the world in terms of a single, observable natural substance was unthinkable to the Babylonians who inscribed in cuneiform, on clay tablets, the myth of Marduk, king of the gods, who brought into being both Babylon and mankind, and who oversaw the destiny of all. Thales' cosmogony and cosmology – that is, his account of the origin and nature of the universe – explained everything the creation myths did, but with reference to a natural, rather than supernatural, principle.

From such beginnings grew a distinction between science and philosophy: whereas experimentation, natural law, and prediction gradually became the life-blood of the former, questions of the greatest degree of generality became the concern of the latter. *What is the basic substance which lies beyond all the phenomena of the world? What are* truth, beauty, goodness, virtue, justice, honour, freedom? *What is the relation of soul to body? What is the nature of gods, if they exist, and is there a life after death?* And, most importantly: *What is the meaning and purpose of life? What constitutes the good life for human beings, and how is it possible to live such a life?* Or, to put it another way: *How can one live a* philosophical *life?*

As reason and experiment began to supersede the faith which marks a predominantly mythical view of life, all such questions came to be approached from a rational perspective. This rational attitude is an integral part of what characterizes both philosophy and science today, just as it distinguished the philosophy of the early Greeks, who called everything into question.

But it would be a mistake to view ancient philosophy as merely an ongoing discourse without any relation to the lives of the philosophers themselves. On the contrary, ancient philosophy was first and foremost an existential choice, a practical choice of a way of life, of a mode of being-in-the-world; but with each choice came also a discourse which examined and justified that choice in the face of criticism from within and without, and which sought to explain the world and man's place in it.

A central part of the purpose of *Stargazers* is to convey this sense of philosophy as a *modus vivendi*, a way of living: that is, in other words, not so much as something one *does* as something one *is*, though in truth both are integral to the way of life known as *philosophia*, the "love of wisdom."

The Period of Ancient Philosophy

Stargazers takes the reader on a journey from the pre-philosophical and pre-scientific myths of the earliest civilizations to the first philosophers – the *physikoi*, or natural philosophers, of the city of Miletus – and through the growth and development of a philosophical tradition in ancient Greece, in which various "schools" arose, flourished, and declined – Ionian, Pythagorean, Eleatic, Socratic, Academic, Peripatetic, Sceptic, Epicurean, Stoic, and Neoplatonist, among others – though not without each having influenced the thought of its time as well as that of thinkers yet to come.

The stories of the philosophers are preceded by two brief sections. The first, "Creation," is an account of the Babylonian creation myth as it was embodied in the New Year Festival at Babylon, an example of pre-philosophic cosmogony and cosmology illustrating the significant gap between mythical and philosophical thought. The second, "The Jewel of Ionia," is a sketch of Miletus, the birthplace of western philosophy and science, bringing into view some of the factors present there, during the century of Thales' birth, which provided the grounding for philosophy's gradual emancipation from myth.

The rest of the book is a series of portraits, in roughly chronological order, of the main philosophers of the ancient Greek tradition and its continuation in the culture of Rome: those intellectual pioneers whose thoughts, words, and deeds reveal to us something of their lives and of their world, and also, to a great extent, illuminate the path of future philosophy both as inquiring discourse and as a way of living.

The tales of the philosophers begin with Thales (c. 600 BC), generally considered the western world's first philosopher and scientist, in whose indifference to wealth and fame, and consequent devotion to his stargazing and to his quest for the principle of all things, one recognizes a way of being-in-the-world that is distinct from that of normal religious and secular life. His whole existence is, in a word, *philosophical*. He does not, any more than did Pythagoras or Plato or Aristotle, engage in philosophical discourse as a mere abstract exercise: on the contrary, his life and discourse are one. This is true, even more so, of later philosophers of the Graeco-Roman period, such as Marcus Aurelius and Epicurus, for both of whom philosophy was, before everything else, the *therapeia* which leads one to the *eudaimon*, or flourishing, life. And it is also true of Plotinus (d. AD 270), the last great figure of Graeco-Roman philosophy.

Thus, the lives of the first philosophers, as much as their words, remain as inspiration and background to our own encounter with philosophy.

Women in Ancient Philosophy

Although the story of the first philosophers is primarily about the *men* who speculated on the origin and nature of the universe and of humanity, and who attempted to live a life in accord with their philosophical understanding, there were a great many *women* in ancient times who devoted themselves to philosophy. The seventeenth century writer Gilles Ménage claimed to have discovered sixty-five women philosophers in his investigation of the works of ancient writers. We certainly know from ancient sources that women were active in the major philosophical schools: those of the Pythagoreans and Epicureans, for example. The singular woman philosopher who is given a chapter in this book is, perhaps, the most famous of these: she who taught Socrates "the art of eloquence" — Aspasia, daughter of Axiochus of Miletus, mistress of Pericles of Athens.

Plato's Dear Delight

There are many ways to become acquainted with philosophy. One way is simply to start at the beginning, to examine its roots and to watch as the first buds appear, to see it flower and, hopefully, to begin to understand something of the nature of its growth and development, as well as its relation to ourselves.

Stargazers is an invitation to return to the beginning, extended cordially to all, but most especially to those who have yet to discover Plato's "dear delight," philosophy. The quest begins and ends in wonder, and, along the way, reveals its power to transform both our perception of the world and our mode of being in it: in short, to make philosophers of us all.

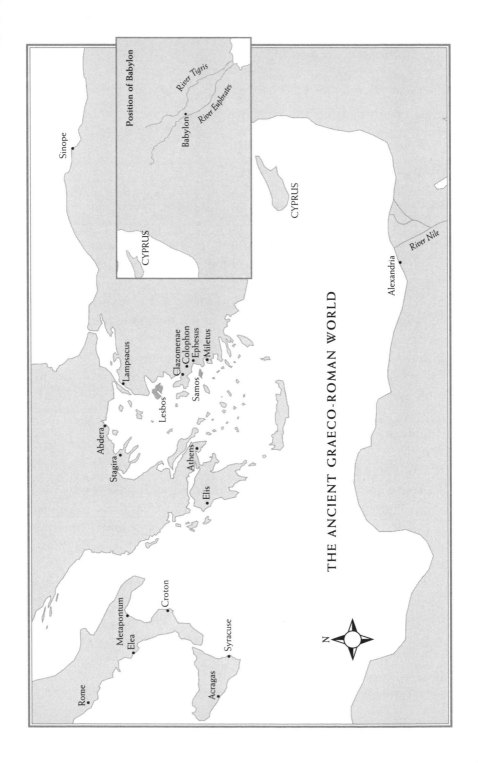

THE ANCIENT GRAECO-ROMAN WORLD

Position of Babylon

River Tigris

River Euphrates

Babylon

CYPRUS

Sinope

Lampsacus

Clazomenae

Colophon

Ephesus

Miletus

Lesbos

Samos

Abdera

Stagira

Athens

Elis

CYPRUS

Alexandria

River Nile

Metapontum

Elea

Croton

Rome

Acragas

Syracuse

N

I
CREATION

In Babylonia, from the third millennium down to Hellenistic times, we find a New Year's festival which lasted several days. During the celebration, the story of creation was recited and a mock-battle was fought in which the king impersonated the victorious god.

H AND HA FRANKFORT

Prelude

The epic poem Enuma elish *("When on high") belongs to a family of Ancient Near Eastern myths which are among the oldest literary works in the world. Inscribed in Akkadian cuneiform on seven clay tablets, the poem dates from about the middle of the second millennium* BC, *though the original composition probably derives from the Old Babylonian period, earlier in the second millennium* BC. *The* Enuma elish *was associated with the annual Babylonian New Year Festival, the most significant event of each year for the Babylonians. In order to reconcile the 354-day lunar calendar with the solar year, knowledge of which was essential for agricultural life, the Babylonians inserted at the spring equinox an eleven-day festival between the end of one lunar year and the beginning of another.*

On the fourth day of the Festival the Enuma elish *was chanted in the evening, and was probably accompanied by pantomime battles whose purpose was to influence the gods and thus ensure success in the coming year. The central figure of the poem is the Babylonian god Marduk; its themes are origin, universal order, renewal, and destiny. In the ritual accompanying the recitation of the*

1

Enuma elish, *the king assumed the role of Marduk and battled the forces of chaos in order to preserve cosmic order.*

The Babylonian New Year Festival was a manifestation of pre-philosophical and pre-scientific thought: the cosmos was confronted through human imagination as a "Thou" devoid of impersonal laws which regulate it, a "Thou" which comprehends and responds to appropriate ritual actions carried out by humans. Such a world view is far from that of the first philosophers. Yet, as with all myth, there is truth within; such truth, however, is expressed not as philosophy or science, but as poetry.

CREATION

Babylon, c. 1400 BC

It is the vernal equinox, time of the annual eleven-day New Year Festival. The everyday life of the city has come to a standstill; during the last four days the priests have performed rites of expiation for the sins of the Babylonians. Meanwhile, the citizens of this great city have mourned constantly: Marduk, king of the gods, is captive in the mountain.

It is the evening of the fourth day, and the priests now recite the Hymn of Creation, the *Enuma elish*:

> *When on high, heaven was not yet named,*
> *Nor did the earth beneath bear a name,*
> *And the primeval Apsu, who begat them,*
> *And chaos, Tiamat, the mother of them both —*
> *Their waters were mingled together,*
> *And no field was formed, no marsh was to be seen;*
> *When of the gods none had been called into being,*
> *Nameless, no destinies ordained;*
> *Then were the gods created in the midst of heaven.*

It is the fifth day of the New Year Festival. The king enters the temple of Marduk, where the high priest strikes his face and strips him of his royal attire. The king falls to his knees, pleading innocence and disavowing injustice during his reign, whereupon the priest performs the rite which restores the monarch to his former status, assuring him of Marduk's favour in the coming year. The people still mourn the disappearance of their god. As chaos reigns in the streets, they ask, "What has become of Marduk? Where is the king of the gods?"

It is the sixth day. Barges begin to arrive at Babylon from surrounding cities, laden with statues of patron gods and goddesses. In the streets, pantomime battles take place as the forces of order struggle to overcome those of chaos.

It is the seventh day. Marduk is at last released from the mountain by his son Nabu, patron god of Nippur, who thereby fully unleashes the power of the forces of order.

It is the eighth day. Within the temple the statues of the patron gods and goddesses are arranged according to their importance, under the king's supervision. The king assumes the role of Marduk and battles Tiamat, leader of the forces of chaos, and her demon followers. After a fearsome display by Marduk, the enemy flees, except for Tiamat, with whom Marduk battles alone. He throws over her a net, which is held down by the four winds, and into her open mouth he shoots the arrow which pierces her heart.

Standing over his vanquished foe, Marduk savours his victory as the north wind carries Tiamat's blood to distant places. Marduk then splits her body into two parts, positioning one half to form the sky, the other to form the earth. From Tiamat's saliva, he creates clouds; from her head, the mountains. From her eyes flow the Tigris and Euphrates, rivers which at once threaten and sustain life throughout the land of Babylonia.

When order has been created in the universe, Marduk hardens the earth so that the house of the great gods, the city of Babylon itself, can be built by the other deities. Then, with the blood of the demon Kingu – he who instigated the conflagration – Marduk forms men and women, whose purpose on earth is to serve the gods well. And from Kingu, Marduk claims the Tablets of Destiny so that he, monarch of the gods, might fix the Fates for the coming year.

It is the ninth day. The king and priests lead a procession of the statues to the Festival Hall on the outskirts of Babylon, where Marduk's victory is announced and celebrated.

It is the tenth day. The victory banquet is over and the procession returns to the city. At night Marduk, the king, takes in marriage a maiden, a goddess.

It is the eleventh day. Now that the forces of order have vanquished those of chaos, the statue-gods assemble with Marduk to determine the Fates for the coming year.

It is the morning of the next day. The New Year Festival is over. Marduk, resurrected, reigns supreme in the universe once again. Thus it is that the gods, the sky, the earth, and all things on it have been created out of primeval waters. Thus has order emerged from chaos. Thus have the gods built for Marduk the temple of Babylon, where mankind, Marduk's creation, might serve them. And thus has Marduk established the sacred rites by which man might gain his favour and thereby prosper.

Nature is renewed and daily life resumes its familiar pattern in all the cities of Babylonia. Ploughing of land and sowing of seed begin another year in Babylon, the chosen temple of the gods, over which Marduk and his appointed representative, the king, continue to preside.

II
THE JEWEL OF IONIA

In Ionia the art, science, and literature of Hellas were born. If Ionia was
ahead of the rest of the Greek world, it owed it to contact with more
ancient civilizations. Ionia learned much from the East, but transformed
its spirit so as to create something which was truly Greek.

AUGUSTE JARDÉ

Prelude

*It may seem almost natural to associate ancient philosophy with the Greek
polis, or city-state, of Athens, especially during the "Golden Age" of that famed
city, and with such immortal names as Socrates, Plato, and Aristotle. However,
it was in the Greek cities of Ionia, on the coast of Asia Minor — particularly
in the city of Miletus — that both western philosophy and science first arose late
in the seventh century BC. True, there were also philosophers at about the same
time in both India and China, and one can certainly find philosophical strains
in early Egyptian and Sumerian writings — the famous moral "Instructions"
of the Egyptian vizier Ptah-Hotep to his son, for instance — as well as in the
Vedas and Upanishads, but the philosophic and scientific tradition which
came to exert the greatest influence over the western world from antiquity right
up to the present time had its origins in the ancient Greek hinterland, which
today forms part of the western coast of Turkey. It was here, on the eastern shore
of the Aegean Sea, that conditions prevailed which were to give rise to views
that would have astonished the Babylonians, whose destiny lay entirely in the
hands of the greatest of gods, Marduk. Miletus, called by Herodotus "the jewel
of Ionia," is the acknowledged birthplace of western philosophy and science.*

THE JEWEL OF IONIA

Miletus, c. 600 BC

The air and climate of Ionia are perhaps the finest anywhere, and Miletus is the region's most ancient and beautiful city, its ornament. In an age of expanding commerce, therefore, it is only natural that Ionia's foremost city has given birth, through colonization, to many other cities throughout the known world, as far away as Scythia and Egypt. It was Megarian colonial initiative that stimulated Miletus to plant settlements along the shores of the Euxine ("Hospitable"), or Black Sea: Sinope, Trapezus, Abydos, and Cyzicus. In partnership with Erythrae, she founded Parion; with Clazomenae, Cardia. It is through these that she now enjoys a virtual monopoly of trading activity on the Black Sea.

Miletus lies on a peninsula some two miles in length and little more than half a mile in width. Two enormous marble lions stand guard over the entrance to the splendid northeastern harbour, the shores of which are lined by three rows of wharves and porticoes. Overseeing the safe shelter offered to Milesian sailing vessels is the sacred shrine of Apollo Delphinios – "Apollo of the Dolphins" – who fulfils his traditional role as guardian of sailors and harbours. The city's abundant merchant ships are further safeguarded by a strong navy. Miletus is indeed a city possessed of many considerable advantages for a colonial power.

And there is a word to encapsulate the life here: *trade*. This city, where all the channels of sea and land intersect on their way to the ends of the world, is animated from morning to night by the bustle of commerce: the multilingual chatter of the marketplace, the movement of crowds of buyers and sellers, the sturdy donkeys that come and go with their precious loads.

In order to nurture her trade, Miletus has developed industries – weaving, dyeing, and embroidery, all learned from the Lydians – the products of which are highly coveted at Athens. Daily, Milesian ships are loaded with woollen cloth, carpets, and ornate vases destined for Scythia in the north, Sybaris in the west, Egypt in the south, their exit from the harbour accompanied by a tattoo of shipwright's hammers busily fashioning yet more seagoing vessels. Milesian wool is exchanged for flax from Colchis, steel, silver, and slaves. Caravans carrying Milesian goods wind eastward through mountain passes toward Babylon, Persia, even India. So pervasive is the influence of the city that presently Milesian traders are preeminent throughout the markets of the Mediterranean.

Like other great towns of Ionia, such as Ephesus and Phocaea, Miletus is animated not only by the bustle of commercial activity of merchants, money lenders, craftsmen, sailors, slaves, and stevedores, but also by a multitude of languages, religions, and customs. One can witness at Miletus Phoenecian sailors performing rites in honour of their god Melkart while Greeks from distant Aegean isles offer a sacrifice to Poseidon for having granted them and their cargo safe passage yet again; and besides these, one may hear many unfamiliar languages and observe many other practices at first strange to the Milesians but now commonplace.

The taste for the luxurious – elaborately decorated vases, exquisite fabrics, ornate jewels – that reigns throughout Ionia is paralleled by an abundance of lively festivals and sumptuous banquets, and all such voluptuousness has become incarnate in the beautiful courtesans of Miletus, who, far removed from the arduous world of the peasant women and slaves whose labour helps to feed and clothe them, are paragons of elegance and refinement.

And so it is that here in Miletus all the conditions required for transcending myth and magic have come together. The fruits of the Agricultural Revolution and the Iron Age have been fused with borrowings from the Near East and remoulded to suit the ever-growing needs of a maritime economy. Here the commerce and trade of the city have become as important as the agriculture of the countryside.

Growing productive powers at Miletus include a large slave population and have brought new classes to prominence. Thus have arisen not only a powerful group of merchants, artisans, and mariners, but also financiers and shipowners. Together they challenge the power of the landed military aristocracy and priests in a continuing and often intense struggle. Presently neither side has achieved complete and lasting victory. There is some consolation, however, in the relative stability which exists under the rule of Thrasybulus the tyrant, who weaves a course between the conflicting demands of the aristocratic and democratic parties.

With the advancement of trade and commerce have come new laws and refined systems of weights and measures. What the Milesians do not develop themselves, they are not afraid to borrow from others: from the Egyptians and Babylonians mathematics, astronomy, mythology, and medicine; from the Lydians the coined money that enables some men, in a surprisingly short time, to amass great wealth and, along with it, considerable political power; from the Phoenicians an alphabet which, adapted to the Greek language, has stimulated abstract thought and the formal study of grammar, as well as having led to the widespread literacy which has ended once and for all the priests' monopoly on learning.

Milesian society is bold, unafraid of the new and often strange ideas which daily infiltrate to challenge the old ones – along with products, mariners, and merchants from other lands, as well as those of Miletus on return voyages. Here is a city in which ideas are exchanged freely, putting to the test the widest variety of views and opinions concerning everything in the cosmos, even the cosmos itself. This is a mercurial society, fascinated by the very fact of change, growth and decay, birth and death. Increasingly sceptical and curious, it hovers precariously on the border of myth and science.

In this most progressive, cosmopolitan centre of the Greek world, it is not surprising that there are those who have become a little bolder than others, a bit more detached from tradition and everyday life. Some of these are fortunate enough to be able to ignore, for the most part, the internecine struggle for power among contending classes, and, instead, to devote themselves to less worldly pursuits. For them, it is not the drudgery of slave labour that is a major concern, nor the daily problems of those farmers whose work sustains the very flesh of the Hellenes, nor the unquenchable thirst of an ambitious few for riches and power.

Their purpose consists in the quest for knowledge of the universe, of the self, and of the secret of the *eudaimon*, or flourishing, life. Indeed, they themselves live a life that is quite different in kind from that of the rest of humanity. And it is they alone who are ready to make the brave leap from *mythos* to *logos*, from poetic myth to rational philosophy and science. Such a one is Thales, the sage of Miletus.

III
STARGAZER

Water is the *arche*, or basic principle, of the world.

THALES OF MILETUS

Prelude

The first philosophers of the western world, the Milesians, are usually referred to as physikoi, *or "natural philosophers." Science and philosophy had not yet been differentiated, and these thinkers took as their province all of nature, seeking the unity behind the diversity of things — the* arche, *or first principle, of all phenomena. Each found the* arche *in a different substance, and it seemed natural to identify the fundamental principle as one of what later became generally recognized as the four elements of the world: earth, air, fire, water. For Thales, one of the Seven Sages of ancient Greece, not only did the earth rest, disc-like, on a vast sea of water, but the* arche *itself was water; for Anaximenes, the* arche *was air. For Anaximander, however, it was* apeiron, *the "unlimited," which accounts for all change, including the multiple forms of the four elements.*

Thales probably chose water on the basis of his experience, shared with the rest of mankind, of a world in which water is of paramount importance: it is ubiquitous, changes form readily, and nourishes all life. The fundamental significance of water for the origin of the world is also evident in early creation myths such as the Enuma elish, *as well as in both the* Upanishads *and the* Bible. *However, it is not the choice of water* per se, *but rather the choice of a natural, observable substance as the* arche *of the world that moves Thales away from mythology toward philosophy and science. For Thales the world*

11

can be explained without reference to the gods; the arche *alone is sufficient. In abandoning mythical in favour of naturalistic explanation and in seeking the unity behind diversity, he opens the pathway to science and becomes at the same time the western world's first known philosopher.*

STARGAZER

Miletus, c. 560 BC
It is midnight, and Thales is walking through a farmer's field as he often does after dark. He never ceases to marvel at the beauty of the heavens. Yet his is not the uncomprehending wonder of other men: Thales has studied the stars for a lifetime. Tonight they are especially beautiful, as there is no moon in the sky to steal their brilliance. He trudges on, oblivious to the undulations in the field, captivated by the mysteries locked in endless galaxies. As he walks, he studies the seven-starred Pegasus, high in the eastern sky, and remembers how the mighty winged horse carried Bellerophon to slay the fire-breathing Chimaera, part lion, part goat, part serpent. It is well known in Miletus that Thales once travelled to Egypt, where he added to his already great store of mathematical learning. From the Egyptians he discovered how it is possible to measure the height of the pyramids. When a person's height and shadow are equal in measure, so will the pyramid's height equal its shadow. One has only to measure the shadow.

Besides having learned from the Egyptians, Thales has introduced a new idea of his own into the mathematics of the ancient Greek world: *proof*. He has demonstrated, among other things, that the opposite angles formed by the intersection of two lines are equal in measure; that an angle inscribed within a semi-circle is always a right angle; and that an isosceles triangle contains two equal angles opposite its two equal sides.

And Thales has advanced knowledge in many other fields, too. As a geographer he explained how the annual Nile floods are a result of trade winds blowing against the river current. Thales the engineer diverted the River Halys to enable King Croesus of Lydia to cross with his soldiers. Thales the statesman advised the Ionian cities to set up a common government at Teos in order to coordinate their resistance against the Persian threat; he also opposed an anti-Persian alliance with the Lydians. Thales' wisdom saved Miletus.

Thales is history's first scientist, and his pupil Anaximander is already carrying on his work, writing the first scientific treatise, *On Nature*, as well as developing a theory of the evolution of living things and drawing a map of the world. But Thales himself is above all else a *philosopher* – though he does not know this word – for he has asked the question which will puzzle humanity through ages to come: *What is the One, the* arche *or principle of the world, that which lies behind all the different forms we perceive in our daily lives?*

Thales has searched for the One from which all things come, and he has found it in water: not water as goddess Tiamat or god Apsu, but water as *natural* element. Like the Babylonians, who each year recited during their great Festival the epic poem *Enuma elish*, he finds the source of all things in water; unlike them, he leaves Marduk out of his explanation. Thales does not so much worship as observe. His object of study is not the gods; it is nature.

All things, Thales says, come from water, including the earth itself, which floats like a giant disc on a vast sea of water. Is it not natural that water, the most abundant substance over the whole earth, should be the basic element of the world? Does it not change readily from solid to liquid, from liquid to vapour, and back again? And is it not required for the nurturing of all life?

But let us add here that already a dialectic has begun, a complex give-and-take dialogue amongst Thales and his disciples. Anaximander, whose bright, unorthodox clothing elicits expressions of surprise from onlookers during his discourses, insists that the infinite "unlimited," or, as he calls it, *apeiron* – not earth, air, fire, or water – is that from which all things come into being and into which they ultimately return; Thales' pupil Anaximenes, on the other hand, says the principle of all things is air, which through rarefaction becomes fire, and through condensation is transformed into water, earth, and even stone or metal.

A *natural* substance, not a supernatural one, is the principle of all things, according to Thales and his disciples, though this does not mean that the gods do not exist. Thales says the gods are in everything. Witness how iron is moved by the magnet, how all things in the world constantly move and change, and how humans have the power of will. Everything is therefore alive, infused with soul, and yet, of all things, it is nonetheless water that constitutes the *arche*, the fundamental principle, of the world.

Thales is the first thinker to speak of his search for the One, and to teach that it is possible to know the world through observation and the power of human reason. He says it is even possible to *predict* the course of events by seeking their *causes*. Did not Thales himself amaze the citizens of Miletus when, with his knowledge of Babylonian astronomy, he predicted the great eclipse which, a mere twenty-five years ago, blotted out the sun and put an end to the fighting between the Lydians and the Medes?

Thales has advanced human knowledge in many fields, and his wisdom is already legendary throughout the Greek world. It is not surprising that he is called *sophos*, or "sage," by the citizens of Miletus. Moreover, Thales' wisdom is practical. It was once said that those who become philosophers do so only because they can't earn money like others. Using his knowledge of the stars to predict a plentiful harvest, Thales proved this to be a lie. He leased all the available olive presses well before harvest time, and when the predicted abundance arrived, there was a great demand for the presses, which he rented out at a considerable profit, quickly amassing a fortune. In this way he showed that philosophers could become wealthy if they chose to. However, the prudent realization that wealth is of little value prevents them from choosing this path.

Although he asks many questions about the world and about people, Thales also enjoys answering questions. Ask him what is most difficult in life and he will reply without hesitation: *To know oneself.* Ask him what is easiest in life, and Thales will answer wryly: *To give advice to others.*

Pegasus is especially brilliant tonight. Thales soars upward to the heavens, like Icarus, to meet him. Fortunately there is no sun to melt his waxen wings. Thales feels himself floating in space, moving ever closer to the winged horse, then suddenly tumbling in a slow-motion free fall, the constellations spinning out of control.

A soft, cold wetness breaks his fall and he splashes about, as if trying to swim. He has not landed in an ocean on some remote planet of the universe: he has fallen headlong into an irrigation ditch where he now stands, water dripping from his robes, his musings temporarily disrupted as he struggles to comprehend what has happened. He finds his predicament neither humorous nor annoying – merely a brief and inconvenient hiatus in his stargazing.

It is July, and the night air is warm. Rather than feeling chilled, Thales finds the water pleasantly refreshing, sharpening his vision of the star-strewn sky. In a few moments he has forgotten the incident and is walking again, intoxicated once more by the haunting beauty of the heavens, seeing in the endless clusters of stars a myriad of figures...an athlete...a goddess...a scorpion...

IV

TRAVELS OF THE SOUL

All souls are kin to one another.

PYTHAGORAS OF SAMOS

Prelude

Pythagoras, whose life is shrouded in legends, was born on the Greek island of Samos. He probably visited Egypt, and possibly Babylonia. In about 532 BC, he left Samos and settled in Croton, which became the home of the Pythagorean Society. Croton was one of the cities of Magna Graecia, or Great Greece, founded on the Italian peninsula between the eighth and sixth centuries BC by Greek colonists. These cities possessed good harbours and rapidly became prosperous trade centres, enhanced by a flourishing agriculture that supplied local needs and produced a surplus for export. Here Greek philosophy was marked by an increasing concern with religious problems and a shift in focus from nature to man — that is, from physics and astronomy to ethics.

The Italian colonies abounded in mystery cults, and it is generally acknowledged that Orphism, the cult of Orpheus, is the most likely source of the Pythagorean conception of the immortality and transmigration, or reincarnation, of the soul. Orphic practices are also the probable source of the rites and secrecy of the Pythagorean Society, as well as of the supreme authority of the leader: "He himself said it" was a common appeal in both Orphism and Pythagoreanism.

Above all else, Pythagoreanism was a distinct way of life, a culturing of the soul through askesis *or spiritual exercises — physical, mathematical, musical, and psychological — including meditation, dietary proscriptions, daily bathing,* communal meals, and doctrinal discussions. Although its genuine contributions to mathematics and science are a matter of contention, Pythagoreanism clearly influenced the philosophy of Plato and, even more so, that of Plotinus and the Neoplatonists.

TRAVELS OF THE SOUL

Croton, c. 510 BC
As he walks, Pythagoras recalls how the new god came to the island – a radiant, golden god who was neither Apollo nor any of the Olympians. The new god was manifest in the form of small, shiny bits of metal. This god moved rapidly about the countryside and had great power, doing much more for some men than the old gods could do.

Polycrates, for example, rose from furniture builder to shipbuilder before becoming tyrant of Samos, from which position he profited greatly through the piracy engaged in by his naval fleet – none of this with the help of the old gods, whom he had long ceased to solicit. And Polycrates was not even of noble birth. It seemed as if the old gods had forsaken the aristocrats in allowing men such as him to prosper. The truth, though, was simply that Polycrates had won the favour of the youngest and most powerful of gods: *Money*.

It was thus that Pythagoras of Samos, having returned from travels to Egypt and other lands, where he had learned of many strange mysteries and rites, came to leave the island of his birth. He lacked a taste for luxury, unlike Polycrates' court poet, Anacreon; nor had he trusted the pirate-king, knowing well the tyrant's intolerance of ideas hostile to his own ambitions. And so Pythagoras settled in Croton, where he proceeded to establish the Society which bears his name and which now numbers some three hundred members. When Pythagoras arrived here, Croton was already well-known for its famous medical school and as the home of Democedes, who left to become physician to Polycrates at Samos. It was also the city of Milo, the famous athlete who reputedly built his great strength by lifting a calf each day until it had become a full-grown bull. Nowadays, however, it is neither the great physician nor the victorious Olympian who elicits sighs of wonder as he passes through the streets of the city, but the saintly Pythagoras. There are even some who claim to have seen his golden thigh when once he pulled aside his robe in the theatre at Olympia. What else would one expect of Apollo's son? For Pythagoras is surely not the son of Mnesarchos the stone-cutter, as others say.

The sage himself has answered the question. When the god Hermes offered him a gift, he chose remembrance of things past. And so he now recalls perfectly his former lives: first as Hermes' son Aethalides; then as Euphorbus, wounded by Menelaus during the Trojan War; then as Hermotimus, during which lifetime he gave evidence of his former existence by identifying Menelaus' shield at the temple of Apollo at Branchidae; and then as Pyrrhus, a Delian fisherman. He also remembers various visitations of his soul to the bodies of plants and animals as well as to Hades, where he learned of the torment all souls there must endure. Presently he lives to the fullest his incarnation as Pythagoras, the sage of Croton.

If all of this is not proof of his saintliness, then why did the River Nessus welcome him? (There are some who actually heard the river hail him as he crossed it!) And how did he come to be seen in two cities at the same instant? Furthermore, it is common knowledge that Pythagoras learned to perform miracles from his first teacher, Pherecydes. We might also ask who else can so readily make of another a true friend. If these things do not establish his godlike nature, then one need only witness his vast learning, which exceeds that of all mortals. Already Pythagoras' name is associated with the most famous mathematical theorem in the ancient world: that the square on the hypotenuse of a right-angled triangle equals the sum of the squares on its other two sides.

The sage is presently on his way to the villa of Milo, where meetings of the Pythagorean Society are often held. Since gaining control of the city and drawing up its present constitution, the Pythagoreans have increased their following and enjoy much adulation. Indeed, they have already proven in several cities, including Croton, that their rule is truly an aristocracy of the best. (It is also true, however, that there is a tide of resentment – even envy – among certain sections of the citizenry.)

Pythagoras is a *philosopher*, a "lover of wisdom" – it is said that this word is his own invention – and he has practised the supreme exercise of seeking and living in accord with wisdom. This, he says, is the true purpose of life. His teachings concern *number*, the *cosmos*, and the *soul*. Number, he says, is more real than the sensible things of everyday life; number is beyond space and time: "All things are number," he affirms. Thus, from numbers we may readily construct everything in the universe. One is a point; two, a line; three, a plane; four, a solid. The sum of these critical numbers is ten, the perfect number, symbolized by the sacred *tetractys*:

Furthermore, not only bodies in space but *all* qualities and relations in the cosmos are numbers: knowledge is one; opinion, with its double edge, two; harmony is three; justice is four, the first square number; marriage is five, the sum of the first even and odd numbers (the number one being neither even nor odd); and so on. Therefore, if we wish to know the nature of things, we must study numbers. This is the central principle of Pythagorean *mathemata*, or knowledge.

There is yet something else, however, underlying number: the ultimate principles of *limit* and the *unlimited*. The very cosmos, and everything within it, arises from their interaction (as well as from other related dualities, among which are odd/even, male/female, unity/plurality, and light/dark). Thus, when we draw a triangle, we must of necessity place a limit on an unlimited plane by drawing three lines which enclose a definite area. All things that exist are likewise a manifestation of these two conflicting principles out of which harmony, order, and beauty arise as a consequence of a limit being imposed on the unlimited – just as a musical scale is the orderly result of placing a limit on the vast, unlimited range of sounds.

In fact, it was from studies of the intervals on a musical string that the Society of Pythagoreans first learned of the dependence of harmony on number. The ratio of string lengths for an octave is 2:1, for fifths 3:2, and for fourths 4:3; adding the different numbers in the terms we have $1+2+3+4=10$, precisely the terms and sum of the sacred *tetractys*. Music itself is simply harmony made audible, says Pythagoras. Harmony extends beyond music, however, for there is an order not only of sounds on a string but of all things in the universe, including the human soul. Thus we can see many instances of harmony in the affairs of society: health, justice, and virtue, for example, all depend on avoiding extremes, on following what is best – the *mean*, or the middle way.

As for the cosmos, its structure reveals perfection in the ten entities which revolve in circular orbits about a central fire: the counter-earth (whose shadow we see on the sun and moon during eclipses, but which we never see itself), the earth, moon, sun, five planets, and the fixed stars. Furthermore, both the universe and the earth are spherical in shape. And surprisingly, the ratios of string lengths for the octave, fifth, and fourth in music apply also to the orbital periods of the planets. The motions of the ten heavenly bodies along their orbits produce wonderful musical sounds, the Music of the Spheres, which we cannot hear because this perfect celestial harmony is constant and unvarying. The universe, therefore, is like a lyre with ten strings, each singing sweetly in harmony with the others.

The *soul*, too, Pythagoras says, is subject to the law of harmony. We may neglect or culture our soul, as we choose. A harmonious soul is one which gains a proper relation to the divine, which relation may be obtained only through such spiritual exercises as *silence, music*, and *mathematics*, as well as through observance of the rules of the Society. The resultant harmony of the soul prepares it for release from the cycles of reincarnation. Philosophy is thus a way of culturing one's soul in order to become freed from the wheel of rebirth and to merge with that divinity from which we have all come. Philosophers, therefore, are not at all like the buyers and sellers at the stadium, nor like the runners who strive for victory, but rather like the observers who calmly watch. This third type, the Pythagoreans say, is best and suggests the superiority of the *bios theoretikos*, the contemplative life, which by imitation of the gods moves one closer to them. By studying the underlying rational structure of the cosmos, which is discoverable in the dialectic of number and harmony, the human soul becomes increasingly rational itself, thereby emulating divine reason.

The questions Pythagoreans put to themselves at the end of each day also contribute to culturing the soul: *What things have I done wrong today? What good have I accomplished? What have I left yet undone?* The answers to these questions give shape to the following day's actions.

The Society of Pythagoreans is a brotherhood of like minds – yet one which, surprisingly, includes women – and its ceremonies and learning are guarded secrets. (It has been said that Hippasus' drowning was the result of his having revealed the secret of incommensurables: the discovery that there are numbers which are neither natural numbers nor ratios of natural numbers to each other – the number $\sqrt{2}$, for example.) It is well known, though, that the Pythagoreans favour a vegetarian diet and that they share in communal fashion all that they possess. It is also common knowledge that they adhere to a host of oral teachings, or *acousmata* – literally, "things heard" – many of which appear strange, even incomprehensible, to the uninitiated. While some are injunctions against certain behaviours, others tell what a thing is, or what is the best or most of something:

- Never eat beans.
- Do not stir the ashes of a fire.
- Do not break bread.
- Upon arising, roll up the bedclothes and smooth out the impression made by the body.

- Don't walk on the highways.
- What are the isles of the blessed? *The sun and moon.*
- What is the Delphic oracle? *The tetractys.*
- What is the most just thing? *To make a sacrifice.*
- What is the best thing? *Happiness.*

Some say that each rule is a divine revelation and has a secret meaning known only to the members of the Society. Perhaps this is so, for there is much else that is secretive about the Order. For example, when Pythagoras lectures to the hundreds who have gathered to hear him, he does so unseen, from behind a curtain. Only when one has been with him for five years is one allowed to look upon the face of the Master.

*

The bustle of this commercial centre of some 60,000 inhabitants greets Pythagoras head on as he passes the noisy waterfront where Ionian goods arrive by ship before being sent off to Gaul and other destinations. Trade here has continued to increase steadily, and the Pythagoreans' prestige has reached its zenith – particularly since Croton's recent victory over its chief rival, Sybaris. Mingled with the usual raucous sounds of commerce this morning, a plaintive wailing – strangely familiar – strikes Pythagoras' ears. Alarmed, he quickens his pace and winds his way through the crowded streets, choosing the most convenient detour in order to arrive at the source.

Suddenly a long wail pierces Pythagoras to the core. As he rounds a corner he witnesses at first hand the cause of one soul's distress. A wild-eyed man is beating a dog with a stick. The creature cowers helplessly, its ears flattened against its head submissively, pleading for respite as its assailant readies to strike another blow.

Pythagoras seizes the man's arm, holding it firmly with a grip that belies his age. "Throw away your stick and never beat this dog again!" he commands sharply. "I knew his voice when first I heard him cry out. It is that of an old friend whom I once knew in a previous life."

A scornful sneer begins to take shape on the man's face as he turns to resume his task, but in the same instant he is struck by the realization that the one who still holds his arm firmly in his bony hand is Pythagoras the sage. The man's demeanour softens and he drops the stick, swearing never to beat the dog again.

Perhaps he fears Pythagoras' miraculous powers. Or could it be that he has heard of Pythagoras' recent conversations with a bear, or has witnessed the sage preaching to a group of dogs? Some men laugh at these tales, but the Pythagoreans see nothing unusual in them, for they know that the souls of men frequently inhabit the bodies of animals. This, explains Pythagoras, is simply a stage in the soul's struggle to free itself from bondage to the body.

Pythagoras continues on his way to Milo's, content in having spared a friend unjust agony, yet at the same time apprehensive about the future of the Society at Croton. Already he senses the coming of violent attacks against Pythagoreans by the envious Cylon and his supporters, and even envisions his own flight to Metapontum, where he will spend his remaining days.

It is a pity that the Sisters of Fate did not grant Pythagoras the full gift of foresight, with which to see, many years hence, the Cylonians burning Milo's villa, and perhaps recognize the few who escape the inferno. Even confronted with such a revelation, Pythagoras might still manage a sardonic smile, for though his body will die in Metapontum, the flames intended to extinguish his influence will serve instead to scatter his ideas to all parts of the Greek world. Thus will the great sage pass, though his thoughts remain, and, sublimated in the philosophies of Plato and Plotinus, continue to puzzle those who seek to know the nature of the real and to live a life in accord with that knowledge.

V
GODS OF THE OXEN

There is one god, greatest among gods and men, similar to mortals
neither in shape nor in thought.

XENOPHANES OF COLOPHON

Prelude
Xenophanes of Colophon was born in about 570 BC and lived to at least ninety-two years of age. He journeyed widely throughout the Greek world, gaining a reputation as an accomplished after-dinner singer whose songs recounted tales of travel and philosophy. About forty fragments of his writings on poetry, ethics, and cosmology are extant, about half of which are from his philosophical poem On Nature. *Xenophanes wrote in iambic elegiac verse, in a style both witty and caustic, mocking among other things Pythagoras' mystical belief in transmigration of souls. He was also a severe critic of popular religion, attacking the blatant anthropomorphism of the polytheistic religion of his time; he counterpoised to it a conception of a single, omniscient and omnipotent, non-anthropomorphic god. According to Aristotle, Xenophanes' god is Nature, not Spirit, and hence Xenophanes is to be regarded as a natural pantheist. The supreme tranquillity of Xenophanes' god reappears two centuries later as a key element in the theology and ethics of Epicurus.*

Xenophanes regarded wisdom as far more important than force or the much-admired physical prowess and athleticism of his time, though he stressed that wisdom is approachable only by long and arduous effort, and that ultimate truth is never fully knowable. The sceptics considered Xenophanes to be a forerunner of their school, as he was also of the satirical genre. Significantly, Xenophanes was the first known western philosopher to advance a conception of One Being, which was to become the cornerstone of the philosophy of Parmenides and the Eleatics.

GODS OF THE OXEN

Syracuse, c. 500 BC
It is winter. The fire is warm, the couch soft. It is not a night to be without a place to stay, especially if one is as old as Xenophanes. It is fortunate that his host has offered him and his faithful servant lodgings. There are others of the aristocrats who, having perhaps heard rumours of Xenophanes' impieties, might not be so accommodating. But there are some who look on Xenophanes as a wise teacher, respecting his many years of travel throughout the land of Hellas.

The gleaming floor and the wine cups and the hands of the guests are clean. The smell of wine and flowers and frankincense perfumes the air. And in the centre of the room the heavy table is laden generously with breads, cheeses, honey, vegetables, and fruits. A libation and prayer are followed by feasting, singing, dancing, and a merry-making as befits the nobles of this fair corner of the Greek world.

The wine and chick peas are sweet after the hearty feast, and the guests, relaxing on soft couches, are all eager to hear a story.

"You are a long way from home, Xenophanes," the host declares. "Tell us, minstrel, of your travels, of what you have seen and of what you have learned," he entreats. "Indeed, tell us, old man!" shouts a chorus of revellers in unison.

"Very well, gracious host and friends," replies the grey-bearded one, rising from the couch to take in hand his lyre. "I'll do better than tell you a tale; I'll *sing* you one," he says, smiling.

Xenophanes strums the lyre and begins a song which, among those present, only his servant's ears have heard before.

When I began my travels over the great land of Hellas,
I was but twenty-five years old.
For forty-five years now have I wandered,
my soul tossed about, my heart filled with care,
and much wandering yet have I to do.
Born was I at Colophon, in Ionia, sweet land of
Thales the Sage, from whence – after its conquest
by the Persian Harpagus the Mede – I travelled
to Messina and Catena, and many other places,
before journeying to Syracuse. My only companions
two in number, you see before you...

Here the minstrel indicates his servant, who nods politely in acknowledgement. Xenophanes smiles as the guests look about the room for a second companion, then in mild perplexity towards the old grey-beard, whose eyes brighten as he holds aloft his lyre to the jovial laughter of the crowd.

"You see now, my friends, that companions need not look just like us," Xenophanes says, sweeping his arm in an arc about the guest-filled room, "but it helps if they can sing – like this!"

He plucks the strings of the lyre to more laughter as the host eagerly urges the poet on with, "Come, Xenophanes, sing us what you have learned!"

"Very well, kind host," the old man replies. "More you shall have, though there be far too much for one song. But let me sing you first a tale of the gods."

O, were we to believe the words of Homer and Hesiod,
we should think the gods no better than men,
with all their faults, for in many ways
the Olympian gods are just like us.
This is natural, for men shape their gods
in their own likeness. This is why the
Ethiopian gods are black with flat noses,
the Thracian gods white, with grey eyes and red hair.
If only oxen and horses had hands –

they would surely draw pictures of their gods
as oxen and as horses!
Yet no man truly has understood nor ever will
understand the divine.
But I sing to you that there is one god —
greatest among gods and men,
similar to mortals neither in shape nor in thought.
He sees and knows all things, is all-powerful
and immovable, utterly tranquil, and has set
all things into motion with his thought alone.

The eyes of some of the guests have opened wide in amazement at the strangeness of the minstrel's canto. This does not surprise Xenophanes, for he knows the ways of mortals. He has borne the fury of some who have reckoned his words too blasphemous; yet he has met enough of the others who have listened with a kindly ear to his tales, and such are the majority present in the room tonight. So he continues to sing.

The strangest part is this: that even if a man
should speak the truth concerning the gods,
he would not know it to be the truth,
for seeming is sealed by Fate upon everything.
Still, mortals can make discoveries about some
things, but only by long and patient inquiry
can they glimpse what is true, and what is best.
Let them therefore state all things as conjecture.

Let me sing now of other stories, of
Homer's multi-coloured goddess, Iris,
whom we see in the sky when the rain
and sun meet.
I sing to you that she whom we call Iris
is but a cloud — scarlet and purple and
green to our eyes — nothing more.

And let me sing of Thales, who said that
water is the arche *of all things.*
He should have said water and earth,
for all things do come from water and earth,
even the soul.
Nor does the earth rest on water, as the Sage
of Ionia said, but beneath our feet goes down
to infinity.

Let me sing of the One Being that is
the universe itself...

Xenophanes continues his song; the guests are transfixed as they listen to the tales of this wandering minstrel who stands before them, strangely calm as he sings of a world that at once excites and frightens them.

Tomorrow he will leave this hospitable villa with his two faithful companions. His host will wish him well and perhaps even say, "May Zeus forgive your kindly-meant transgressions." Xenophanes will smile graciously in return, but as he walks away he will already be thinking of the many places he must yet see before he sleeps.

VI
FIRE AND FLUX

You cannot step twice into the same river, for new waters are ever
flowing upon you.

HERACLITUS OF EPHESUS

Prelude

*Heraclitus was born late in the 6th century BC into an eminent family in the
Ionian city of Ephesus, which, like the rest of Ionia, was under Persian rule
during his lifetime. Resigning a hereditary priestly-political office in favour
of his brother, Heraclitus dedicated himself thereafter to philosophy. Nobody's
pupil, he gained his wisdom through self-inquiry, conscientiously following, it
would seem, the Delphic oracle's dictum:* Know thyself.

Heraclitus' book On Nature *apparently consisted of sections on the
cosmos, politics, and religion. The surviving fragments and doxographies –
histories chronicling the views of the ancient philosophers – reflect Heraclitus'
concerns with a wide variety of subjects: other thinkers, such as Homer, Hesiod,
Pythagoras, and Xenophanes; the nature of human knowledge; metaphysics
– the nature of ultimate reality, the eternal flux, and the unity and struggle
of opposites in all things; science, religion, ethics, politics, and psychology.
Although some of Heraclitus' fragments are relatively easy to interpret, many
are difficult and therefore remain the focus of much contention.*

*As a result of his style of speaking and writing, as well as his despair over the
sad state of his fellow citizens, Heraclitus gradually gained various nicknames
– "Obscure," "Riddler," "Dark," "Weeping" – and his name attracted many
spurious stories concerning his manner of living. When asked about Heraclitus'*

book, Socrates declared that what he understood was excellent, and, furthermore, that what he did not understand must be excellent, too, even though it would likely take a skilful diver from Delos to get to the bottom of its meaning. In spite of the difficulties Heraclitus presents, however, his fragments continue to be of great interest to students of philosophy and science.

FIRE AND FLUX

Ephesus, c. 490 BC

Heraclitus has just written the final words of his book *On Nature*, which he plans to hide in the Temple of Artemis, one of the great wonders of the world, before he leaves the city forever. He will go into the mountains and take up a life of contemplation, living on herbs and roots. By hiding his work, something of his hard-earned wisdom might be preserved for future generations. This, Heraclitus thinks, is far better than wasting his learning on the Ephesians, for, he tells us, they are as uncomprehending of his words after hearing them as before. What else would one expect of those who are willing to believe the folksingers and follow the mob as their teacher?

Presently he is taking counsel as he does infrequently, and only, with the one whom he trusts.

✳

"Why am I seeking counsel? Because I have had enough of the rule of mediocrity, and since it is of no use to speak to the mediocre citizens of Ephesus, I speak to you."

You are angry, Heraclitus. That is obvious.

"Should I not be so, after the Ephesians have turned out Hermodorus, the best man among them, one who was worth ten thousand of the others? They could not stand to look each day upon a man far better than any of them. The Ephesians deserve to be hanged, every last one."

Is this judgement not overly harsh? They are only mortals, after all.

"Yes, that is true. And it is evident that the gods need not envy any of them, though they may perhaps feel a kinship with the few who are like Hermodorus. The Ephesians are living proof that most men are by nature bad. Nor are they possessed of any good sense whatsoever, no matter how great their learning. When I speak to them, though they are in my presence, they are completely absent."

You think poorly of your fellow men, Heraclitus.

"Most are like beasts satisfying themselves at the trough; only the few who are best choose to be known for worthy acts. The Ephesians think that always having what they desire is the finest thing; but this is the expectation of fools, for whatever the soul wants, it buys with soul. Those who are wise have learned to control desire and to direct it toward that which accords with reason, that same reason whose highest expression is in God."

Perhaps the Ephesians do not understand you because you are too difficult. You know yourself that they sometimes complain of your obscurity. I, of course, understand you, but not always without great effort.

"You do not complain about the oracle at Delphi, who shows the god's meaning by a sign. Just as one must make many journeys in the struggle to be good, one must work hard to find Nature's secrets, for She loves to hide from men. One's eyes and ears are false witnesses if one's soul does not understand. Nature speaks to those who are willing to listen: those who pay attention to their senses and to the fire in their soul, their reason."

Yes, I know. Perhaps you would have been better off had you lived with those such as Pythagoras and Xenophanes, or Homer and Hesiod.

"They all had much learning and little sense, and did not know that learning alone does not produce wisdom. As for Homer, he deserved to be thrown out of the games. And Hesiod did not even know that day and night are one and the same, just as the sea is at the same time most pure and yet most polluted: for fish, life; for humans, death."

You are a severe judge of mankind. What of the great sage Thales, who showed us the arche, *or principle, of the world?*

"He showed us, but he was wrong. It is not water that is the *arche*, but fire. For it is fire which is most capable of change and motion; it is fire which is an exchange for all other things just as all things are an exchange for it. Fire is want and surfeit, conflict, birth, death. The world is a *flux*, a flow of continuous change – which itself is the *only* constant – the same for all, not made by men or gods but always having been, and ever to be, living fire, kindled by measures and quenched by measures. Even soul consists of measures of fire and water, the dry part of soul being highest, bearing within itself the fire of reason, the wet soul of a drunk being the lowest.

"Fools think that all would be better if there were no such change, but without change there would be no world. Homer, who prayed for the end of strife unwittingly prayed for the end of all things, for it is by strife that the world exists. War is the father of everything! Without evil we would not know good; without hunger we could not experience satiety; without pain, what meaning could pleasure have? And so on. As strife leads to generation, peace leads to conflagration and destruction, just as stillness precedes the storm.

"A good symbol for all of this is the bow, whose name *bios* means life. The drawn bow, its wood and string in tension with one another, represents life with its unity of conflicting forces, some generative, others destructive; yet the function of the bow is to bring death."

In the past, I have had trouble understanding how this interchange takes place.

"There is a *Logos* which lies beneath the manifold appearances of the world and through which fire becomes all things and all things become fire, in an eternal war of opposites. The One is Many and the Many are One. Earth to water to vapour to fire: this is the upward way of *rarefaction*. Fire to vapour to water to earth: this is the downward way of *condensation*. The sea and earth are the great source of the exhalations which rise and gather in 'bowls' – their hollow sides toward us – in the sky, and flame into heavenly bodies. It is the varied exhalations in conjunction with the movements of these bowls which account for day and night, the phases of the moon, eclipses, the seasons, and changes in weather.

"All things, including human beings, are governed by the *Logos*, the heart of the flux; it alone is permanent and gives permanence to the world. This is all written down in my book. The Ephesians will not understand a word, of course, but perhaps some day others will..."

I think you expect too much from life, Heraclitus. You have always lived comfortably enough, even after renouncing your hereditary priestly office in favour of philosophy. Why can't you be happy like other men?

"Is a cow happy when she finds grass to eat?"

Not happy, perhaps, but –

"There is nothing more to say on that subject. Happiness is more than bodily pleasure, which is something rather easy to acquire. Much harder is to see men following those such as Hermodorus, whom they have cast out instead.

"The highest excellence is temperance, and the wisdom of man consists in living a life of moderation, speaking truthfully, and acting with a correct understanding of Nature. Wisdom comes from understanding the *Logos*: one must strive to comprehend the nature of things and the coherence which underlies them; this alone is the way to live rightly, since humanity is part of the cosmos and is therefore likewise steered by the thunderbolt. However, although the *Logos* is accessible to all, few achieve understanding because they live as if asleep in a private world. Most men do not notice things when awake, just as they forget what they have done while asleep."

Sometimes I think you need to counsel with God, Heraclitus, rather than with me.

"And what is God? The masses pray to statues of gods, but I ask whether it makes sense to speak to a house when its dwellers are absent?"

Of course not, but surely –

"The mysteries they practise are unholy mysteries, purifying themselves with blood as if stepping into mud to cleanse themselves. They do not know that to God all things are right, for good and evil are one, just as life and death are one. And although war may seem a terror to us, to God not even war is terrible, for He makes all things contribute to universal harmony. Just as without hunger we should not know satiety, without evil we would not know good.

"God is day and night, summer and winter, war and peace, life and death. God is to man as man is to a child; God is the one wise thing, both willing and unwilling to be called by the name of Zeus – willing because He is God; unwilling because He is utterly unlike the mob-made gods!"

The Ephesians asked you to write a law code for them. You refused.

"The city has already been mastered by an evil constitution. I would rather play dice with children than politics with the Ephesians. Children have more sense than their elders, for they are as yet uncorrupted by them. But at least I have warned the Ephesians to hold fast to their laws and to guard them as they do their city walls, for their laws are the common possession of all and take their nourishment from the one divine law."

It is not too late to make your peace with the citizens of Ephesus. Leaving the city for a hard life at your age will not be easy.

"This you know to be true: the Ephesians dislike me almost as much as I detest them. In any case, it is not worth sacrificing the soul for an easy life. No, I have made my decision, and after placing my book in the temple, I will leave the city of my birth."

✳

Heraclitus rises and, taking in hand his mighty work, he walks one last time to the temple of the Huntress. The counsel has given him clearer sight, with which he views in the distance the mountains of his new home. And so it is that Heraclitus the Obscure will continue to confide in the one he knows best and trusts, the one whom only those like Hermodorus can call their peer: Heraclitus himself.

VII
THE GATES OF
NIGHT AND DAY

Reason shows us what the senses do not – the true nature of Being.

PARMENIDES OF ELEA

Prelude

Parmenides, perhaps the most difficult and controversial of all Presocratic philosophers, was born late in the 6th century BC into a noble family in Elea, a southern Italian refuge for exiled Phocaeans after the Persian conquest of 542 BC. At first Parmenides followed the Pythagorean Ameinias, and may have studied with Xenophanes. His followers were Zeno and Melissus, and he deeply influenced Anaxagoras, Empedocles, and Plato, and therefore all of western philosophy.

The philosophy of Parmenides is expressed in his hexameter poem On Nature, *recounting his journey from ignorance to knowledge. Some one hundred sixty verses survive, including the "Prologue" and most of "The Way of Truth," which depicts the nature of ultimate reality. "The Way of Seeming," of which little remains, apparently gives the most satisfying account of the illusory world of sense-experience, a world hitherto taken for granted by Ionian thought. Parmenides thus counterpoises the reality of the* intelligible world of truth, *known through reason, to the illusory* perceptual realm of opinion. *It seems clear that he is rejecting both the Pythagorean fusion of opposites in the mean and the Heraclitean struggle of opposites. His poem abounds in references to the ancient Mysteries and seems more like a truthful account of an actual mystical experience than an allegory.*

In focussing on the true nature of Being, Parmenides thus introduces into philosophy the realm of ontology, *and in distinguishing sharply between appearance and reality, he revolutionizes* epistemology, *the theory of human knowledge, and prepares the way for the opposing strains of Platonic idealism and Democritean materialism.*

The central message of Parmenides' poem is that Being, the One, is, change, or Becoming, is illusion. He leaves philosophy with the task of reconciling these.

THE GATES OF NIGHT AND DAY

Elea, c. 480 BC

Prologue

The wise mares carried Parmenides to the ends of his longing, escorting and guiding him to the illustrious god-path upon which tread men of understanding.

Led by maidens, the mares glistened as they strained at the chariot, its axle whistling and glowing brightly in its socket, huge wheels spinning at its ends. The Daughters of the Sun fled from the house of Night and, throwing back their veils with their hands, led the philosopher toward the light of Day.

Then it was that Parmenides saw the gates of the paths of Night and Day, enclosed by a lintel and a stone threshold, and fitted with two great doors whose keys are kept safe by Justice herself. With honeyed words the maidens beguiled her into opening wide the doors, whereupon they guided mares and chariot onto the broad way which lay before them.

Justice, sweet goddess, took hold of Parmenides' right hand and said, "It is Right and Justice which have set you on this road with your mares and immortal charioteers. Here shall you learn all things, both the unwavering heart of Truth and the false opinions of mortals, in which we can place no trust."

The Way of Truth

And the goddess Justice continued to speak of the unrelenting heart of Truth to the philosopher Parmenides.

"There appear at first to be two roads of enquiry: one into that which *is* and another into that which *is not*. Yet there is but one account of Being – and that is the story of what actually *is*. This path alone can we follow, and the many signs along the way speak to our Reason about the true nature of Being.

"Do not yield to custom and the perceptions of the senses, as do those undiscriminating crowds of mortals who, carried as if by a river, sail past Truth unaware, believing *that-which-exists* and *that-which-does-not-exist* to be both the same and not the same, as have those philosophers who claim that all things are mixtures of opposites: good and evil, light and dark, hot and cold, moist and dry.... Reason shows us what the senses and the opinions of mortals do not – the true nature of *that-which-is*, the true nature of Being.

"First, know that *nothing* does not exist. Hence, we cannot think of *that-which-is-not*. If we cannot think of it, how can we speak of it? And if we cannot speak of it, then we cannot inquire into *that-which-is-not*. Thus, only one way remains: *that-which-is*.

"And as to the nature of what is, firstly it *is* and *cannot not be*, for if it can be thought of, it can be, and if it can be, it is. Whatever exists always was and always will be.

"Can we say of Being that it has been generated? How could this be possible? If something comes to be, it must come to be out of Being or not-Being. Did it come from what is not? No, for this is entirely unthinkable and unsayable, and therefore impossible. Even so, we cannot imagine what necessity could have generated Being from nothingness.

"Or shall we say that it came from what is? But in that case, it already was, and so it remains ungenerated.

"As for dissolution, does a thing pass from what is into what is not? This would make identical *that-which-is* and *that-which-is-not*, but the latter has no existence, nor can it even be spoken of."

Justice pauses for a moment, allowing the philosopher to grasp the meaning of her strange words, then continues. "It must also be said of what *is* that it is One. For if it were Many, it would have to be divided. But divided by what? If Being is divided by Being, then Being remains continuous, and hence undivided. On the other hand, we cannot say that Being is divided by non-Being, since non-Being, or void – empty space, nothingness – does not exist.

"And what of motion? The common opinion is that it exists in all phenomena. But if there is motion, there must be void, or non-Being – space, in other words – through which things can move. But Reason says there is no void, only Being.

"Furthermore, it must be said that Being is *complete*, for nothing exists but *that-which-is*. Thus, Being, fettered in chains and held within its limits, is completed fully on all sides as a perfectly round ball, like the earth itself.

"Know, Parmenides, that there are two worlds in which we may live: that illusory world of Appearance given to us by the senses and founded on the false opinions of mortals concerning what is and what is not: a world of change, generation and dissolution, a world of Many.

"And then there is the other world, a world of Reality, which Reason alone shows us: a world consisting only of Being, a world that is One, and it *is*, and it is impossible for it not to be."

✳

And here the goddess broke off her words and bade the philosopher follow her onto the Way of Opinion, that he might see more clearly the folly of the common opinions of mortals, and the deceitful reports of the senses, so that no mortal mind may ever again beguile him.

Thus came Parmenides to know for the first time the true nature of Being, which is shown to man not by the senses, nor by the opinions of the undiscriminating crowd, but by the light of Reason.

It is true that men *sense* change, motion, plurality. They direct the movements of their own bodies, witness motion and change, observe an abundance of individual objects, and speculate on the causes of such things, *as if* they were real, but all these phenomena are based on the evidence of the senses, which constitutes a grand illusion. Yet it is an illusion in accordance with which the unthinking multitude live their lives, utterly blind to Truth. Reason alone shows us unequivocally – as the goddess has revealed to Parmenides – the nature of Being: finite, complete, ungenerated and indestructible, motionless and unchanging, spherical. Being is One, and it alone *is*.

It remains for Zeno of Elea, Parmenides' most famous disciple, to demonstrate with ingenious arguments the stillness and oneness of Being.

VIII
ARROWS OUT OF TIME

> Zeno's arguments about motion, four in number, cause great trouble for
> those who attempt to solve them.
>
> ARISTOTLE

Prelude

*Zeno of Elea, son of Teleutagoras, was born in about 490 BC. A pupil and friend
of Parmenides, he succeeded his teacher as the leading figure of the Eleatic school.
The world of seeming, or opinion – the world of the senses – was subjected to
Zeno's logical powers, and his work consisted in trying to show through a series
of aporiai, perplexing problems leading to contradiction, that plurality and
motion are inconsistent notions which ought to be rejected as illusory. Thus,
he was a defender of the motionless and ungenerated Parmenidean One. Of his
forty aporiai, only nine have come down to us: four against plurality and five
against motion.*

*Zeno is generally regarded as the inventor of dialectic, the question-and-
answer technique used to inquire into the nature of things. This method was later
made most famous by Socrates, who as a young man was deeply influenced
upon hearing Zeno speak at Athens. In a sense, Zeno may also be regarded
as the father of logic, for he took Parmenides' argument and subjected it to a
systematic questioning and analysis in order to demonstrate its truth. In doing
so, he prepared the ground for Aristotle's wide-ranging study of the modes of
human thought and his development of formal logic.*

*Accused of involvement in a conspiracy to depose the tyrant Nearchus at
Elea, Zeno was arrested and thrown into prison. It is said that before he was*

killed by the tyrant's men, he bravely endured torture, thereby demonstrating his utter indifference to both pain and death.

ARROWS OUT OF TIME

Elea, c. 450 BC

The tall and handsome Zeno has accompanied Parmenides on a journey from Elea to Athens for the festival of the Great Panathenaea. Parmenides carries the Eleatic hope of gaining an alliance treaty with Pericles, but for Athenian philosophers the chance to listen to Zeno is paramount. Among the guests tonight at the home of Pythodorus, just outside the city wall, where Zeno and his mentor are staying while in Athens, is the young Socrates. He, along with several others, has been eager to hear Zeno speak about his writings.

Zeno's work contains a series of *aporiai*, or problems, whose solutions consist in *reductio ad absurdum* proofs: Zeno begins by assuming a point which everyone seems to regard as true, and then he demonstrates that the assumption in question involves a contradiction, an absurdity. All forty of his *aporiai* have been included in his book and continue to create quite a stir wherever Zeno goes, especially when the philosopher himself reads or recounts them to audiences.

✳

Zeno is presently telling the guests about a race between Achilles and a tortoise.

"Consider this, my friends — a race between the swift-footed Achilles and the sluggish tortoise. Achilles, swiftest of runners, can surely defeat the tortoise rather easily. Yet reason shows us that not even Achilles is able to catch up to a tortoise who has been given a head start."

The guests look at each other, perplexed at the outrageous suggestion which is utterly contrary to their common-sense notions. Even though most have already heard of Parmenides' rejection of motion, hearing it from the lips of his famous pupil has renewed their initial surprise and confusion. Zeno continues.

"Let us agree that Achilles begins at a starting point A, just as the tortoise has already reached a point B, ahead of him. It follows that by the time Achilles reaches point B, the tortoise, who is in continuous motion – however slow it may be – will already have advanced to a further point, C. By the time Achilles reaches C, the tortoise has moved further on, to D. As Achilles reaches D, he notices the tortoise ahead of him, at E. And so on.

"As the race wears on, Achilles is clearly approaching the tortoise, moving ever closer, and yet he can never catch the tortoise, for each time he reaches the point at which he previously saw the tortoise ahead of him, the tortoise has moved on to another point. This, as logic reveals to us, will go on without end, for no matter how many times Achilles reaches the point at which he previously saw the tortoise ahead of him, the tortoise will have advanced still further."

Zeno pauses to survey the varied expressions of wonder and bewilderment which his words have wrought, before continuing.

"Now, you may object that all the spectators in the stadium can actually *see* Achilles catch the tortoise, pass him, and win the race, and that this evidence of the senses settles the matter conclusively. This would be easy to establish were Achilles still alive today, though in fact any swift runner would suffice to make short work of a tortoise in a race. The problem, however, is that all of this begs the validity of sense-perception itself, which is precisely what we are putting to the test by finding whether or not it conforms to our reason.

"Reason demonstrates Achilles' – or anyone else's for that matter – victory in the race to be an impossibility, a mere sensory illusion. And when sense-perception and reason collide, what are we to think? Well, my friends, it is clearly reason, not perception, which shows us what is possible or impossible. What tells us, for example, that it is impossible to have both a finite and an infinite number of things in the universe? Not our senses, for they cannot enable us to perceive at once the entire universe. No, it is our reason which settles this sort of question decisively. In the present case, considering the situation Achilles faces, reason shows us beyond doubt that the world we perceive with our senses is illusory. Thus, we must rely on reason to tell us what Being is really like: it is *motionless*.

"But you may still object, 'Zeno, you have shown that there is a contradiction in assuming that Achilles can win the race, but you have not convinced us that motion is utterly impossible.' Well, then, let us consider another *aporia* which, I think, will surely leave you convinced."

At this point Socrates interjects a question. "Zeno, I see that you are saying pretty well what Parmenides has said about the universe being One, though you seem to do so in a negative way, telling us rather that there are *not* several things – that there is no plurality. Are you doing this to give a semblance of difference between you and Parmenides, and relying on the fact that all of this may be above our heads?"

"My dear Socrates, you are right in your observation of sameness between Parmenides' position and mine, but please don't think that this is mere word-mongering on my part. You are so good, in spite of your lack of years, at pinning down the meaning of what someone says, I fear you may misunderstand my intention and think that I am setting up *aporiai* in the way I do merely in order to show myself as a clever speaker. On the contrary, that which you mention is simply an incidental aspect of my manner of expression. In truth, I have tried to defend Parmenides' arguments against plurality and motion. The gods know how many have already ridiculed his poem on the grounds that absurd conclusions follow from it, or that it contradicts our everyday experience. But the *aporiai* show, I think, that the denial of Parmenides' position entails even *more* absurdity.

"But now, to get back to my point that motion is utterly impossible, take the example of an archer drawing back the string of his bow. He releases the string and the arrow takes flight. Let us begin once again with an assumption: that the arrow travels from the archer to the target – that is, the arrow moves through a distance. Consider, however, that at any instant during its flight, the arrow is motionless. It is suspended, at rest, completely immobile at any given moment of time we may choose: t_1, t_2, t_3, and so on. Thus, since the time taken for the arrow to move from the archer to the target consists of an infinite series of such instants, just as a line is taken to be composed of an infinite series of points, and since the arrow is immobile at each of those instants, the arrow never moves – for an infinity of nothings still equals nothing – and the archer cannot send the arrow into the target.

"If we imagine the target to be closer to the archer – even exceedingly close – the same argument holds. Thus, our original assumption – that the arrow travels from the archer to the target – involves a contradiction, for the arrow can *never* reach the target. In fact, as reason has shown, it cannot move *at all*. Hence, motion is indeed an impossibility!"

✳

As Zeno finishes speaking, the small crowd of listeners sits in stunned silence, wondering how to make sense of what they have just heard. Has all of Zeno's discourse been an illusion, just like the archer's moving arrow? If so, what is the reality behind it? The guests rise from their seats and begin to discuss what has just taken place, confused and yet excited by the newness of the ideas brought to them from across the Adriatic Sea. Life for them, and for philosophy, will never be quite the same again.

IX
OF LOVE AND STRIFE

Having seen but a small part of life, men, so quick to die, rise and drift away like smoke on the wind, convinced only of that which they have chanced upon while they are driven here and there. Who then can claim to have seen the whole?

EMPEDOCLES OF ACRAGAS

Prelude

Empedocles, son of Meton, son of Empedocles, was born in about 495 BC in Acragas (now Agrigento, Sicily) into a noble family whose fame was all the greater for his grandfather's victory in horse-racing at the Olympic Games of 496 BC. An aristocrat by birth, Empedocles helped to overthrow an oligarchy, though he refused the kingship offered to him by the grateful citizens. He became a leader of the democratic movement in Acragas, but after a political resurgence of the aristocrats was exiled to the Peloponnesus, where he died in about 435 BC.

The philosophy of Empedocles can be seen partly as an attempt to reconcile eternal Being with the apparent fact of change. In his complex philosophical poem On Nature, *he explains how the objects of our experience arise through the interactions of four roots or elements – air, fire, earth, and water – and two fundamental physical forces of attraction and repulsion:* Love *and* Strife. *Another poem,* Purifications, *deals with ethics and the human soul, and with the Pythagorean doctrine of metempsychosis, or reincarnation. Man's fall from moral purity can be expiated through various reincarnations of his soul until he becomes liberated from the cycle of rebirths, though this can be achieved only by consciously striving after wisdom, following the path of reason.*

Empedocles' activities included not only philosophy, but natural science, politics, medicine, poetry, mystical theology, and oratory. Aristotle declared him the founder of rhetoric, and he was the first thinker to propound a detailed rational explanation of the origin of species. Tall tales surround the life of Empedocles, including the story of his jumping into the volcanic Mount Etna and leaving a bronze slipper behind so that he might be remembered as a god.

OF LOVE AND STRIFE

Acragas, c. 445 BC

The sun has passed its zenith and Empedocles is preparing to go out into the city, where he knows he will be met and followed by a throng of citizens. Theirs is an adoration he has earned through noble action based on his belief that wisdom is something to be shared. Empedocles has devoted his life to enlightening others.

Today the sage has donned his purple mantle and gold belt and is wearing his bronze sandals and Delphic laurel wreath, just as he does when he wanders among poor and suffering ones in all parts of the land. He passes through the doorway into the open air, under the endless roof of the azure sky. Already many are awaiting his presence, and as he walks they begin to trail behind him.

Empedocles has proven himself to be a man of diverse talents. He has shown great leadership as a democrat opposed to the self-serving rule of the aristocrats. He is also a poet whose style is renowned wherever his words have been heard, for he is one who, like Parmenides, has expressed his philosophy and mystical theology in hexameter verse. And Empedocles is a scientist who has studied the nature of the universe and of the human body. Above all, however, he is a healer whose name is associated with a considerable number of miracles. At Selinus, did not Empedocles cure the plague caused by river pollution? The citizens remember well how he ingeniously diverted the water of two other rivers into a canal to wash away the disease. They fell to their knees, worshipping him as a god, so thankful were they for such a gift.

And his protection of gardens from a ruinous wind by building a wall of animal skins earned him the title of "Wind Tamer." And who else could bring back from death a woman who, for thirty full days, had neither breath nor pulse? Most incredible of all, however, was his journey to Hades and back again, a magical victory over the shades of the underworld. Yet, would we expect less than this of a divine being?

Reaching the top of a hill, Empedocles turns to address those who have patiently followed him thus far. The man who is at once prophet, poet, healer, and leader speaks to eager ears.

"O, my friends, you who the mighty citadel inhabit which crowns the golden waves of Acragas, you who strive for noble actions: I, an immortal god, no longer a mere mortal, greet you with the same good wishes as those which I meet wherever I go throughout this land. Upon entering a prosperous town I am welcomed heartily and honoured by the men and women who follow me by the thousands, seeking prophecies or healing words in exchange for sickness, or directions for the road to success in a venture close to the heart.

"Friends, know that my stories are true, though I am well aware that trust comes hard and slowly to the human mind, for most choose proof over faith. And if I should repeat myself, bear with me, for it is no mean thing to speak twice of what one should. But come, hear my thoughts, for learning enlarges the mind, and each of you, no matter how far from the gods now, is fully perfectible!

"Let us begin by remembering Thales, the sage of Miletus, who taught us that the *arche*, or principle, of the world is water; and his pupil Anaximenes, who insisted that the *arche* is air. Heraclitus, we know, chose fire as the exchange for all things. But now let me tell you of that which truly gives to us the infinite variety of things we sense in the cosmos, those things which appear to come anew into the world and then gradually decay into nothingness. I shall speak to you frankly of the fourfold nature of Being.

"Know, first of all, that Being can neither arise from non-Being nor perish into non-Being. All those things which seem to do so are not manifestations of a change in Being – neither its creation nor its destruction nor its transformation from one kind of Being to another kind – but rather a different mixture or separation of the components of Being: air, fire, earth, and water. These four are the *rhizomata* – the roots or elements – the true *arche* of the world: they are what constitute Being, and they are ungenerated and indestructible. When they are mixed in a given proportion a specific thing appears to our senses; and when they are separated from that proportion, the thing disappears. A mixture in a different proportion yields a different thing.

"Look for yourselves at the evidence. See the sun, hot and radiant, dazzling to the eyes, and the divine bodies of the great expanse of air, bathed in its brilliance; look at things dark, chilled, and rain-soaked; and notice how, from earth, pour forth the many rooted, solid things. From these come all things that were, are, and ever will be: trees, men and women, animals and birds and water-nourished fish, and gods, long-lived, highest of all in greatness and honour.

"Any named thing in the universe – a piece of wood, for example – is composed of a mixture of all four elements, in a ratio specific to itself. Thus, a piece of wood is composed of the same four elements as, say, a bronze sword, but the relative amounts of the four elements are different for each.

"Do not believe those fools who think that what did not yet exist suddenly comes into Being, or that what once existed has now gone out of Being. For nothing comes out of nothing, nor does that-which-is dissolve into that-which-is-not. Neither does man's true being begin at birth and end at death, for these are simply processes of mixing and separating: *birth* and *death* are merely names given to these things by men.

"Thus, there is change, I say, but not a generation or destruction of Being; rather, the change we perceive is a result of the mixing of the four unchangeable elements of Being: air, fire, earth, and water. They alone are uncreated, imperishable, and unchanging in quality. These are the roots, or elements, of the worldly existence of things, and it is only the composition of their mixtures that alters.

"As to how the changes in appearance take place or, to put it another way, how and why the mixtures and separations of the four elements happen the way they do, we must look to those forces of attraction and repulsion whose work it is to bring about and dissolve worlds such as our own: I speak of Love and Strife. Why would any change occur if there were only air, fire, earth, and water? It is only through mixture and separation, under the influence of Love and Strife, respectively, that the apparent changes in the universe take place; for one kind of matter cannot become another kind by mere condensation or rarefaction, as the Ionians have taught. No, the four roots are unchangeable."

Surveying the crowd of listeners, Empedocles acutely senses their earnest striving after the divine essence of his message. He continues to lead them with his words toward the great cosmological cycle of the world.

"Consider for a moment how a painter mixes from his palette of basic colours a variety of combinations in order to create all possible hues. In just such a manner do Love and Strife bring out of the four roots all the sensible qualities of the cosmos by combining those roots in an endless variety of proportions. The process occurs in phases determined by the relative ascendancy of Love or Strife.

"There are four phases to the cosmological cycle of the world. When Love dominates all, there is the homogeneous Sphere of Parmenides, the One, in which the four roots are thoroughly interwoven. Here there is no cosmos, no living things as we know them, nothing to be distinguished, no void, no motion.

"As Strife, from its confinement at the centre of the Sphere, begins to penetrate Love's dominion, the four roots begin to separate and combine in such ways as to produce a material cosmos filled with living things, becoming in time the world we inhabit.

"Then, when Strife approaches total domination, utterly confining Love and separating the four roots completely, the world and all things in it are destroyed in the ensuing Vortex.

"As Love begins once again to increase its power, gradually

mixing the roots together as before, a cosmos is created and, within it, living forms. Yet not all of these forms are adapted for continued life, for many are strange combinations, such as oxen with men's heads and men with the heads of oxen. These will die out; but those properly suited and fit to survive and reproduce will live: men and women, animals, plants.

"As Love's power reaches its apex, the four roots have become intermixed and indistinguishable from one another in the Sphere. The cycle is at an end, and another cycle of thrice a myriad of years begins. This is the never-ending cyclical process brought about by the powers of Love and Strife. From One, things become many; then from many they become One; and this goes on forever. Now you can see that the things we sense are not everlasting in their sensory form, though the four roots of the world, which give them birth, are indeed permanent. Thus it has always been; thus it is now; thus it will always be, according to the rule of necessity."

Empedocles pauses, allowing his words to settle fully on the crowd. He looks randomly at individual faces among the gathering, striving to grasp what more must be said to bring them that which they long for most of all. He continues.

"But let me speak about our perception of things. Our senses work through a meeting of elements outside us with those in us; effluences from objects enter through the pores of our sense organs, giving us a sensory perception of those things. The size and shape of both effluences and pores are varied, so that only when these match will effluences be able to enter the sense organs. And it is the attraction of like to like that allows all of this to happen: when the effluences from light objects meet with the fire in our eyes, or those from dark objects meet the water in our eyes, we see the objects; and thus it is. Nor are perception and thought ours alone, as most seem to believe: know that all things have intelligence and a share in perception and thought.

"Yet men, though seeing but a small part of life, quick to die, rising and drifting away so soon like smoke on the wind, remain convinced of that which they have chanced upon while being driven here and there, as if somehow they had discovered the whole. However, it is only the intelligent use of the senses in conjunction with what I am telling you that will enable you to achieve the whole. Knowing all of what I have told you, then, trust your senses while keeping always your reason in charge as the master overseer."

A voice from the crowd penetrates the philosopher's hearing, asking how one might learn to live rightly, in order to avoid the pains that lie in wait upon the imprudent. Empedocles responds.

"Friends, come, listen and I will give you that philosophy which is the only genuine therapy for your anguish, for it is my task to pass on wisdom to those I shall soon leave behind for the eternal company of the blessed gods. Know first that in its connection to the body, the human soul forgets from what heights of honour and bliss it has fallen. Just as the human world has fallen from a worship of Love to one of War, so have men and women exchanged the very heavens for an earthly life. For those souls that have erred in swearing false oaths are consigned to wander of necessity far from the blessed ones for thrice a myriad of years, and become throughout time many kinds of mortal, travel many a pain-filled path of life as they move in penance from body to body.

"Strife takes no pity on the souls thus despised and tortured in this world, until at long last Love hastens to bring all things once again to unity. And so it is that birth is a journey abroad for all of us, for we are all strangers and fugitives from the gods. This I know from experience, for I have been such a *daimôn*, banished from the blessed company of the immortals.

"Thus I urge you, fellow Acraganians, first and foremost to abstain from eating flesh, for each man's body is the Strife-made home of a punished soul. The luckiest of souls embodied in animal form are the lions; among plants, the laurel reigns. I myself have been boy, girl, bush, bird, and silent fish swimming in the sea; wise Pythagoras, too, recalled his former lives, and bade us perform those exercises which alone lead to atonement, perfection of spirit, and divine purity. In like manner, all souls pass into the many forms of animals, but the wisest ascend to godhood, highest in honour.

"My fellow Acraganians, we must live rightly in order that our blessedness begin now and continue to increase when we leave this realm, until at last we rest eternally at the hearth of the immortal gods, freed of mortal pain and penance. But now we are here within this roofed cave of the earth, fugitives and wanderers in the darkness, amid a host of plagues.

"So let us not defile our altars with the blood of bulls – the greatest sacrilege of mankind! Let us follow rather the path of wisdom which reason brings us to, in order that we may be filled with peace and contentment: the path of common justice which forbids the killing of animals." The listeners look at one another, nodding and whispering as they recall Empedocles' sacrifice at Olympia of an ox made of honey and oatmeal, a fitting gesture to those who yet defile the altar with living blood.

The philosopher chooses his closing words carefully, that they might be what his listeners remember best. "Go with the gods and keep them before your eyes, in true piety: their stillness, their swiftness of thought that travels in an instant over the entire world, their invisibility, their likeness – and unlikeness – to us. Most importantly, approach them through silent reverence and reap the happy wealth of divine thoughts, but shun always the wretchedness brought by dark beliefs about the gods."

✳

Thus spake Empedocles, descendant of kings, enemy of aristocracy, friend of the *demos*, scientist and sorcerer. The crowd follows the philosopher toward the outskirts of the city, longing for yet a few more soothing words, a healing touch…a miracle.

X
MISTRESS OF
ELOQUENCE

That I should be able to speak is no great wonder…considering that
I have had an excellent mistress in the art of rhetoric – she who has
made so many good speakers, and one who was the best among all the
Hellenes, Pericles, the son of Xanthippus.

SOCRATES

Prelude

*Born in about 470 BC, Aspasia was the daughter of Axiochus of Miletus.
She was educated as a* hetaira, *or courtesan – a woman trained to be a paid
companion to wealthy aristocratic men. A* hetaira *was no mere prostitute, but
rather a woman well-versed in history, politics, science, art, music, literature,
and philosophy. Such a woman was able to enter into the intellectual life of the
polis, normally the domain of men, and to aspire to a degree of independence
unknown to the typically sheltered and ignorant aristocratic women of Athens.
Although Aspasia's status as a* metic, *or resident foreigner, prevented her from
becoming an Athenian citizen – as it did also her son by Pericles, the Athenian
leader – it did little to hinder her freedom as a* hetaira.

*Aspasia began to live with Pericles in about 445 BC, after he and his wife
had divorced amicably. She continued to teach philosophy and rhetoric and
was so famous as a rhetorician that a rumour arose about her having been the
composer of the funeral oration delivered by Pericles after the initial casualties of
the Peloponnesian War.*

*Charged by the poet Hermippus with impiety and abetting prostitution,
Aspasia was saved from imprisonment by Pericles' speech and tears at her*

trial. Shortly thereafter, in the autumn of 429 BC, Pericles died of a pestilence that swept through many parts of Greece, and which was particularly severe at Athens. After the death of Pericles, Aspasia took Lysicles as her protector and, with her knowledge and skill, she helped him to rise to political prominence, though he lived for only a short time afterward. Little else is known of Aspasia's life after Pericles' death; she died in about 410 BC.

MISTRESS OF ELOQUENCE

Athens, c. 440 BC

Tonight's guests have already finished a sumptuous feast of meats, fish, breads, and cheeses, interspersed with the pouring of libations in honour of their hosts, Pericles and Aspasia, and of tonight's speaker, who is their teacher. Presently they sit or recline on soft couches, the tables before them garnished with figs, grapes, olives, and chickpeas, as well as goblets filled with a pleasant mixture of dark red wine and water. The conversation is softened by anticipation of the words of their Master; the wine is sipped slowly.

Aspasia bids the dancers and the players of flute and lyre to retire, as she prepares to present tonight's speaker to the guests, among whom she begins to circulate in order to ensure the completeness of their comfort. Ever since Pericles took Aspasia as his mistress – she would be his wife but for the law, initiated by Pericles himself and passed more than ten years ago, prohibiting Athenian citizens from marrying *metics*, or resident foreigners – she has taken part in affairs of state and has turned his home into a veritable centre of culture, where every day, politics, literature, art, music, and philosophy are discussed earnestly by many of the most creative minds of Athens. Did not Pericles himself, just the other day, have an afternoon-long debate with the sophist Protagoras and several others regarding who was responsible for the accidental death of a javelin thrower that very morning?

Among the guests tonight are the tragedian Euripides, the

sculptor Pheidias, and the young philosophers Archelaus and Socrates. Several have brought their wives along, something which the men who come to hear Aspasia's lectures often do, for their wives do not sit at home spinning and weaving as do so many Athenian women, who remain, as a result, utterly ignorant of affairs of state, art, culture, and philosophy. These women, on the contrary, are fascinated by the rhetorical skill and practical wisdom of Pericles' mistress. "It is she," Socrates recently declared, "who taught me the art of eloquence."

And an excellent teacher Aspasia is, yet not only a teacher but also a highly skilled practitioner of rhetoric. Many recall how she recently demonstrated with great eloquence to Xenophon and his wife that in order to be happy with each other they must become convinced that each is the best possible partner for the other; for Aspasia astutely sensed that without such a conviction, these two would always be in want of that which they consider to be the best and would never be truly happy with each other.

The daughter of Axiochus of Miletus is known by her golden hair, silvery voice, and high-arched, delicate foot – signs of her beauty and charm. In her youth she followed the lead of the *hetaira* Thargelia, seeking out men of power, thereby placing herself in a position to exploit her talents as freely as the male citizens of Athens are able to realize their own. And so she studied history, politics, art, music, and literature – she herself is an accomplished poet – as well as philosophy. In choosing to live with Pericles, she has enabled herself to set for the women of Athens a radical example of both moral and intellectual freedom.

Aspasia gives classes in philosophy and rhetoric, the art of eloquence in speech. When she first came to Athens ten years ago, she opened a school, taking as students young women of good families, and encouraging their higher education and emergence into public life. Let it also be said, however, that her house was, in addition, a home to young courtesans – a fact which has lately given rise to wild rumours concerning her personal life. In spite of this, a number of prominent Athenians regularly attend her classes, including Socrates, Pheidias, and Euripides.

In fact, Pericles himself studied rhetoric with Aspasia, for it was not only her beauty that attracted his eye and heart, but the elegant mind exemplified by her eloquence in speech and her political acumen. That Pericles' fondness and respect for Aspasia has never waned is evident from the fact that each day as he leaves home, and again as he returns, he embraces and kisses her.

As one might expect, Aspasia has been accused of many things by the enemies of Pericles. After all, what better way is there for them to get at the incorruptible leader than to attack those closest to him! Hermippus, the well-known comic poet, has called her impious and insinuates that she procures young girls for Pericles. Cratinus, it is said, has called her a dog-eyed concubine. Eupolis calls her a whore and mother to a bastard, referring to her son by Pericles; here Eupolis means that the boy suffers a similar ironic fate to that of his mother: he is held back from Athenian citizenship by the very law invented by his father.

None of this has disturbed the equanimity of Aspasia, however; nor has it stanched the flow of visitors to the most famous centre of culture in Athens. Pericles continues, undaunted, to oversee the dramatic changing of the face of his city. Pheidias and his army of architects, carpenters, smiths, and sculptors have been painstakingly rebuilding the temples of the Athenian Acropolis after their destruction by fire at the hands of Xerxes and the Persians some forty years ago, using only the finest of the luxurious materials transported into Athens from afar: bronze and gold, ivory, marble, and the exquisite wood of the cypress. The jewel of the Acropolis, the Parthenon, is now nearing completion. The golden-hued marble columns of the temple of Athena Parthenos, the virgin, were designed by Callicrates and Ictinus and are being decorated under the direction of Pheidias. Athens is being transformed before the very eyes of its citizens into the most beautiful city in the Hellenic world.

Along with this transformation of the urban landscape has come a flowering of the arts and culture of this great city. Under Pericles' leadership they have blossomed as in no city anywhere in the known world. The dramatists Aeschylus, Sophocles, and

Euripides have incarnated on the stage of the theatre, with profound artistry, the meaning of the ancient Hellenic myths, transforming them for their own time. The poet Aristophanes holds up to comic scrutiny all things, while the Ionian historian Herodotus of Halicarnassus, who is now living in Athens, has already given several readings from his astonishing account of the Persian wars.

Until recently Athenian culture had never been the equal of that in other parts of the Greek world, but now, under the leadership of Pericles, commander-in-chief of the great Maritime League of coastal cities and islands of Greece, Athens has become the foremost cultural centre of the Hellenic world.

*

Aspasia continues to circulate about the room, exchanging words with guests, from time to time motioning to slaves to bring more wine and water, or grapes and figs. Those gathered here begin to sense that the time has come for her to present the speaker – though, in truth, he needs no introduction, so well-known and revered is he by all present. With the decorum expected of a mistress of eloquence, Aspasia surveys the room filled with eager listeners, waiting calmly for all eyes to be on her, which in but a moment they are. She smiles briefly and then begins to speak, her elegant manner eliciting the admiration that accompanies her everywhere.

"Friends and fellow-philosophers, I shall keep you from your hearts' desire no longer. Our speaker tonight is well-known to all of you, as, like Pericles and myself, you are his students in that way of life known as *philosophia*. Our honoured teacher will speak to us of his philosophy as expressed in his mighty work *On Nature*, which is nothing other than a tale of cosmogony and cosmology – the origin and nature of the universe – of creation and destruction, of the many worlds that exist besides our own, and of the Reason which guides all things.

"He is one with whom both Pericles and I – as, indeed, most of you as well – have had many long conversations, and to whom we are ever grateful for the deepening of our understanding of the cosmos and the world of humankind. Even now as I speak, his book is being read in our city and sells for a mere drachma, a trifling sum in exchange for so much learning. But I shall say no more now, for it is he whom we have all gathered to hear."

*

Aspasia does not mention his name: there is no need to. She turns her head to look over one shoulder, and she nods gently. One of the guests, a man of about sixty years of age, stands up to receive a chorus of exhortations from the gathering. He approaches Aspasia, who embraces him before retiring to her place beside the leader of golden Athens. There she waits calmly, along with the others, in anticipation of the profound wisdom of the one who has brought philosophy to life in Athens: Anaxagoras of Clazomenae.

XI
MIND

In everything there is a portion of everything.

ANAXAGORAS OF CLAZOMENAE

Prelude

Anaxagoras was born at Clazomenae, in Ionia, in about 500 BC. Shunning the practical matters connected with his birthright, he gave away his inheritance in favour of a contemplative way of life. He made significant advances over the work of his predecessors in philosophy, continuing the attempt to reconcile the impossibility of creation or destruction of Being, on the one hand, with the everyday perception of motion and change, on the other. He also advanced science, particularly the understanding of astronomical phenomena. His work provided a prelude to both the atomistic physics of Democritus and the ideal world of Platonic Forms, knowable only by Reason.

In place of Empedocles' Love and Strife, Anaxagoras posits Nous, or Mind, as that which gives birth to the vortex which spins our world into existence. And in place of the four roots of Empedocles – air, fire, earth, and water – he substitutes spermata, *or seeds, the combination and separation of which yield the qualitative diversity of our world. His cosmogony, or theory of cosmic origin, differs from that of Empedocles in being a traditional non-cyclical one, beneath whose observable plurality lies an indestructible realm of Being.*

The life of Anaxagoras at Athens was intimately bound up with that of his famous pupil Pericles. At this time in Athens, however, there was a great resistance to free thinking and to new ideas from other parts of the Greek world,

63

especially philosophical ideas. Accused of impiety in 431 BC, Anaxagoras was imprisoned, but with Pericles' help he managed to escape to Lampsacus, where he lived out the remaining few years of his life. Just before he died, he was asked by the archons of Lampsacus how he wanted to be remembered. "Give the children a holiday," he replied. Apparently, his wish was granted.

MIND

Athens, c. 440 BC; continued from Chapter X

"I, Anaxagoras of Clazomenae, son of Hegesibulus, friend of Aspasia and Pericles, address you now in order to speak of that which constitutes the foundation of our way of life, known as *philosophia*. I speak, therefore, of those very things which Thales and the Milesians sought to explain, and also Heraclitus the Obscure, and Parmenides and Zeno of Elea, and Empedocles of the brazen sandals.

"I ask you those questions which lead us to the *arche*, or principle, of the world. How did things begin, and, once having begun, were they thereafter destructible? Did yet more things continue to come into being? And how are the changes we witness even possible? What can our senses and our reason tell us of such things?

"Let us first look to the beginning. Then it was that all things were mixed together completely, in perfect stillness, a single Entity of the sort Parmenides is reputed to have identified with the world of Being that only Reason can know. Here is where we must seek the origin of creation and destruction, for from perfect stillness how is it possible that motion and change should arise? This is the problem of Becoming, bequeathed to us by the philosophers of Elea."

The guests ponder intently the words of their teacher as he pauses in order to allow them to take the true measure of the problem he has posed. Then he continues to speak.

"From such a beginning in perfect stillness, it was *Nous*, or Mind, the most subtle and purest of all things, that began the movement which brought the heaviest things toward the centre and the lightest toward the periphery, the vortex which created the universe we inhabit. It is *Nous* which is everywhere, possesses complete knowledge of things, as well as utmost power, and is able to direct all. Other things each contain a part of everything else, but *Nous* is pure, unmixed, infinite, and self-ruling. It is its unmixed nature, its purity, which enabled it to initiate the movement of the cosmos, for matter by itself could never have done this. It was Mind that started the great rotation which began to separate things out from an indistinct, motionless mass.

"Yet, how can we account for the formation and nature of the many things we sense around us? It is not the four roots or elements – air, fire, earth, and water – out of which all things are formed, but *spermata*, or seeds, countless in number, infinitesimal in magnitude. These seeds we may also call *homoiomereiai*, or "things with like parts," for although each seed possesses a unique quality, it also contains a portion of all things in the world. Yet one portion within each seed is *dominant*, and therefore the appearance of an object shows to us that substance whose portion dominates the whole. Thus, while a piece of wood contains within its innumerable seeds a portion of all things in the universe, it has the appearance and properties of wood because it contains more of wood than of anything else."

Observing the puzzled looks which tell him that a few of his listeners are struggling to grasp his meaning, the philosopher pauses momentarily, inwardly resolving to express himself in such a manner as will render all things clear to them. He reassures them before beginning to speak again.

"As this account contrasts so strongly with popular opinion, and therefore seems strange and unfamiliar, we must look to *why* it is that everything *must* be in everything, for if we can demonstrate this, then all that I have told you so far will become perfectly clear. Consider, for example, how the bread or grain or cheese we eat results in new growth of hair, nails, muscle, or bone, for it is well-known that food nourishes these things. But how is it possible that what is not-hair should become hair, or that what is not-bone should become bone? Clearly such things are impossible: bread or grain or cheese cannot become hair or bone. And yet, on the other hand, we know that hair and bone are built from such foods. Only one conclusion is possible, and it is given to us not by the senses but by reason: namely, that hair and bone must be present in the bread, grain, and cheese, even though we do not perceive these portions within the foods.

"And so it is with all things, that through the attraction of like to like, new combinations of seeds are formed, always with a dominant portion which is perceivable, the numberless smaller portions of everything else remaining unsensed. There is no such thing as a pure substance, for all is mixture, save Mind itself; nor is there a smallest, for there is always a smaller and it, too, will contain a portion of everything. And behind all the change of the world, Being, alone, remains uncreated and indestructible."

The philosopher pauses again in order to give his listeners a chance to gain a deeper sense of the strange and wondrous nature of their world. The guests take furtive sips of wine and water while keeping their eyes fixed on the man whose words have entranced them. They nod their heads in agreement with those things they have come to understand, furrow their brows in perplexity at those ideas they have yet to make their own. Satisfied, Anaxagoras continues his discourse.

"Now, let us look into the nature of perception and knowledge. Here we find a paradox to be reckoned with, for although it is the attraction of like to like that underlies the combination and separation of things, it is *unlikeness* which forms the basis of our perceptions. Since a portion of everything is in us, we are ready by our very nature to perceive through the meeting of unlike with unlike, each such encounter producing in us a sensation – even a pain – the pain of recognition of *unlikeness*. Thus we sense, by contrast, cold when it meets with heat within us, wetness when it meets with dryness in us, bitterness when it meets with sweetness in us, and so on, each in proportion to our deficiency in that quality.

"But our senses, though they reveal clearly the dominant portions of things – wood in wood, metal in metal, barley in barley

– cannot reveal to us precisely the innumerable lesser portions within things. Yet our reason enables us to imagine far beyond such limits, as we just saw when we established how food must contain within itself portions of hair, bone, flesh, and all the other parts of the body that are replenished by nutriment. Be therefore unswayed by common opinion, but rather use your reason well in conjunction with all you are given through sense-perception, for these, along with your understanding of the nature of things, will give you what you need to live that philosophical life which is our common goal."

Aspasia rises to offer a goblet of water mixed with wine to her teacher. Anaxagoras accepts it and pauses to drink before advancing to his final subject.

"Let me now speak of the importance of the meditation on nature. You all know that I am most at home when looking at the night sky. An Athenian once asked me, after hearing my utterance of a comment critical of the Hellenes, whether I had no respect for my native land. I responded by pointing to the star-strewn heaven overhead, saying, '*There* you see my native land.'"

The laughter of his fellow philosophers makes Anaxagoras halt momentarily, assured that the vastness of his perspective has been appreciated, though he already knows it is one they ever strive to share. He continues to speak of his encounter with the stars.

"My study of the heavens has not been fruitless, for meditation on nature brings understanding. It is my stargazing, more than anything else, which has led me to the discovery of *Nous*, or Mind, as the motive principle of cosmogony, of the formation of our world and its star-filled heavens. Let me share with you some of the many secrets of nature which my investigations have revealed. First, know that for all their beauty the sun and stars are but gigantic stones whose speedy whirling has set them ablaze. The sun is indeed large, bigger even than the Peloponnesus, and very hot. The stars are more distant than the sun, and therefore we do not feel their heat as much. The moon, on the other hand, is but a cold stone which receives its light from the sun. Being closer to the earth, it sometimes becomes interposed between earth and sun, and this interposition and consequent darkness on the earth we call an eclipse.

"On the earth itself, there are many wonderful phenomena which are equally well explained by reference to the natural motions of things. The winds that sweep over the land from the sea, for example, are a consequence of the sun's heat, which rarefies the air and imparts motion to it. A rainbow is merely a reflection of the sun in clouds above the earth. Thunder and lightning are produced by a collision of those same clouds. Deep within the bowels of the earth is trapped large volumes of air whose movement shakes the surface of our planet. And occasionally fragments of burning rock are thrown off from the sun and sink to earth with a streak of light: these are what we call falling stars.

"Such are some of the wondrous things of earth and heaven that belong to our world. Know, however, that there are also other worlds besides ours. Many have their own sun and moon, mountains and seas, houses and trees, animals, and people like us. The moon, I say, is a world in many ways very much like our own. And, gazing at the heavens, we can only wonder how many are the countless other such worlds we may never know."

The day has been long, and Anaxagoras is satisfied that he has said enough. He looks to Aspasia as if to indicate his readiness to end his discourse and rejoin the others, when a guest suddenly asks, "What of death, Anaxagoras?"

"That," replies the Master, thoughtfully, "is a fitting subject with which to close my little speech, for it is regarded as a thing of ultimate finality. Yet, death is nothing more than another change, a separation and combination of seeds. And no matter where we start, we must all travel by more or less the same descent to Hades. As for an end that comes too early, we must remember that from the moment in which we bring about that rearrangement of seeds which constitutes new life, we ensure also that corresponding dissolution and rearrangement which we call death – for who but a god is immortal.

"Thus, while we are able, let us live the life of philosophy and gaze ever upward to the stars, our true homeland."

✳

These are the words spoken by Anaxagoras of Clazomenae, son of Hegesibulus, teacher and friend of Pericles and Aspasia. It was he who first brought to Athens the way of life known as *philosophia* and taught how it was Mind alone which began the ceaseless movement of the world.

XII
MAN, THE MEASURE

Man is the measure of all things; of things that are, that they are; of
things that are not, that they are not.

PROTAGORAS OF ABDERA

Prelude

*Born in Abdera around 490 BC, Protagoras travelled twice to Athens, where
he enjoyed considerable success. He became the most prominent of the Sophists,
sages who took money in exchange for philosophical teaching. Sophism was a
natural consequence of the unstable social and political conditions, particularly
at Athens, during the second half of the fifth century BC. As this period began,
Greece was at the height of its power and Athens was the centre of Mediterranean
power; by its end, Athens had been reduced by the Peloponnesian War to a
skeleton of its former self. In such a time, the skills required for discussion in the
law court and in the* agora *— that place of popular assembly and the market
— were taught for a fee by a collection of philosophers more diverse than their
singular designation, "Sophists," might suggest. The most respected of these
thinkers — particularly by Socrates and Plato — was Protagoras.*

*In their exaltation of reason and scepticism, and in their challenging long-
established traditions, the Sophists were representatives of a period of enlighten-
ment. As such, they were generally regarded as a danger to society. Ironically,
though a product of Athenian democracy, the Sophists' services were affordable
only to the wealthy few.*

*A friend of Pericles and Euripides, Protagoras practised in philosophical
discussion what has come to be known as the Socratic method of dialectic, first*

introduced by Zeno: the question-and-answer technique used by Socrates in Plato's dialogues as a means of getting at the truth about fundamental notions such as knowledge, virtue, and justice.

Extolling reason, scepticism, pragmatism, and the health of the human soul, Protagoras was the first to support himself by philosophy. He died in about 410 BC.

MAN, THE MEASURE

Athens, c. 430 BC

Protagoras and his pupil Euathlus, having met at the *agora*, are engaged in dialogue.

✳

Master, what were you thinking about when I happened upon you? You seemed deep in meditation.

"I was allowing myself to marvel at the idea that – the Persian assault having been beaten back – Greeks are now in control of the Mediterranean. Yet at the same time, I was thinking that the current conflict between the Athenian alliance and the Peloponnesian League, headed by Sparta, may bring on us more trouble than we are presently able to imagine."

It seems you may be right, Protagoras, though I would rather not think about it.

"Well, then, let us move to more pertinent matters, Euathlus. You promised to pay me the fee you owe for your rhetorical training, but I have not yet received it."

And so I shall, Protagoras, though, as you remember, I agreed to pay you after I had won my first case at the law court, which I have yet to do.

"You appear to have been stalling, Euathlus. If you take no case, you cannot hope to win, and therefore you cannot hope to pay my fee. And unless you take a case soon, I may have to give you your first case myself by bringing a suit against you. Of course, I leave it to you to decide whether I am serious in what I am now saying."

If you were indeed serious, good Master, it would be unfortunate, though it would present us with an interesting situation –

"Do you think so? Well, perhaps. In any case, we'll come back to this question, but let me digress for a moment. You have proven yourself to be one of my best students – is this not so?"

I defer to your judgement on that question.

"Let us put it to the test. Do you recall the parts of discourse?"

I do: they are wish, question, answer, and command.

"And the seven basic forms of speech?"

Yes. In addition to the four parts of discourse, there are narration, rehearsal, and summoning.

"You have studied verb tenses?"

I have.

"And you know fully the importance in debate of   "

Seizing the right moment? Yes, I have learned that timing in rhetorical matters is crucial.

"And have you not fared well in the debating contests I have organized for my pupils?"

Yes, very well, for my teacher has given me all the necessary skills of the trade.

"Well, then, you must not put off any longer your true test, by which I mean the court case that will win for you your first public acclaim, and my fee in the bargain!"

The time will come soon enough, though I have no strong wish to rush into it prematurely.

"Prematurely? I have taught you to argue and you have mastered the art of proceeding equally well from either of the two sides of any given position – that is, you can attack and refute any side, can you not?"

I would not yet be so bold as to claim a full mastery of this skill for myself, though for you it seems a natural gift.

"Not so much natural as the fruit of long and patient study, and therefore something available to all in greater or lesser degree."

To you in the greatest degree, I would say, even though your ability in this respect may not be fully appreciated by all Athenians.

"I understand you. Our time is like a sea of strangely conflicting currents, and we must learn to navigate well if we are to find our way to a solid footing. On the one hand, we see the great democracy of the Athenian *polis*, in which every citizen has his say at the law court and the Assembly. This is a freedom which ought to be cherished, and it is one through which Pericles has encouraged the flowering of philosophy. Yet, on the other hand, there are those who would pluck the bud before it flowers, and tear up its roots, for they fear the subjection of all things to the inner eye of reason."

To them you are Reason incarnate, and for this they fear you.

"It is true that they view all Sophists with a hostile eye, for we are not Athenian-born; we are *metics*, resident foreigners. I, as you know, come from Abdera, in Thrace. That such ones as we Sophists dare play teacher to Athenians is hard for them to swallow."

Do they not envy also the plain fact of your success?

"They resent our charging a fee for lessons; yet what choice do we have? Either we exchange our freedom as citizens for a livelihood or we live impoverished."

This they appear to resent most of all.

"Even more do they resent our abilities – yet why should they, for we have said that these are available to all who hire a good teacher and practise well the lessons they are given. We stand ready to offer our services for sale at any time."

The young men with money want your services, though all social classes in Athens resent you.

"We subject their traditions to scrutiny, and thereby threaten that which they cling to most fervently. They fail to see the liberating force of philosophic enquiry, as well as the resultant education which can change a worse condition into a better one."

It is your book about the gods that has placed you in danger. Please, Master, do not forget the fate of Anaxagoras of Clazomenae, another metic at Athens. He dared to call the sun a flaming piece of stone, for which act he was promptly charged with impiety and imprisoned by the Athenians. Your book, I fear, may have placed you in a similar position.

"It was in the house of Euripides that I first read my book *On the*

Gods. Soon afterward a public burning of this work was organized after copies were collected from those who possessed them. The Athenians were deeply alarmed by my opening lines: 'As to the gods, I have no means of knowing either that they exist or do not exist, nor if they do exist of what form they are.'"

You did the unthinkable, Protagoras: you challenged a cherished tradition and thereby became a threat to the very foundation of society and public security. I notice that these same Athenians had no desire to burn your other works, such as On Truth, Antilogic, On Mathematics, *and* Of Ambition. *Clearly your discourse on the gods struck a nerve and caused them a measure of pain.*

"That is true. Yet their tradition does not stand up to reason, for it is but another form of false piety. Its defenders have never thought about how they could possibly know that which they believe they know."

So, then, it is man rather than god to whom we must look in order to know what true piety is?

"Not only piety. As I have said before, man is the measure of all things – of things that are, that they are; and of things that are not, that they are not. One person says, 'It is hot'; another says, 'It is cold.' Both are right, and for the one who is in a state of discomfort, the statement is merely the expression of a need to change a worse condition into a better one; some appearances are better, others worse, though none is truer than any other. We may also say that a given ethical view is better than another, provided we mean only that it is more useful or expedient. And we may say that some men are wiser than others – if, for instance, they can recognize a useful or expedient view or practice – and also that no man thinks falsely."

Then all humans – not only the sage – have access to truth?

"Precisely."

How did you come to know this?

"The older philosophers tried to find the *arche*, or principle, of the world, but we can see how different were the various results of their speculations. Each of the philosophers gave us something, but their conclusions were at odds with one another. What they have shown us is how little we are certain of. It is best to speak of the world we see as merely the sum total of all appearances that it has for all persons.

"Heraclitus was right, though, in one respect at least: things are in a state of flux, of constant change. Given this, we must see how impossible it is to produce an absolute truth, for not only are things changing as we speak, but we, the speakers, are changing too."

How difficult it becomes, then, to find anything stable to hold on to!

"Yes, for truth is not something fixed once and for all; nor should we even think of truth so much, but rather of that which works and, with respect to the individual, that which brings health to one's soul. What seems right and admirable and just for a *polis* is truly so, as long as that general opinion continues to be held. There is no more to it than this. And as for the consequences of such a view, well, look at it this way: if we can change a person's condition from a worse to a better one, that is enough, and to accomplish this is philosophy's unique task. And do not forget, Euathlus, that everyone is capable of learning *arete* − that is, of learning virtue or excellence − for it is already in some measure widespread throughout society; indeed, if it were not, society as we know it could not exist at all.

"Therefore, let us always seek the better over the worse, or, to put it another way, that which conforms to Nature rather than that which conflicts with Nature."

And you have based your teaching on these principles?

"Yes, and I have taught you of mythology, religion, grammar, poetic interpretation and, most importantly, the principles of rhetoric. The latter are indispensable for you in your role as a citizen of democratic Athens in our time."

And this is why you have so many pupils, such as myself, whom you have taught eristics, *or the art of winning an argument, for such rhetorical skills constitute a great advantage. I understand all of this now. A man never knows when others will bring a suit against him in the courts or, conversely, when he will be forced to do the same.*

"I hope you will adhere always to the principles of *arete*, which I have also given you. And remember that one ought to converse differently in disputation and in serious discussion: the one who disputes may have fun tricking his opponent, but the dialectician will be conscientious and will attempt to correct his fellow interlocutor only when he feels it to be absolutely necessary."

You may rest assured on that point.

"Now, Euathlus, tell me: when we consider any problem, what must we ask first of all?"

What is its relation to physis, *or Nature, on the one hand, and to* nomos, *or convention, on the other?*

"Correct. Can you give me an example?"

Is human language merely conventional — that is, man-made — or is it natural? We may also ask the same of human laws: are they somehow given to us by nature or do we invent them? Again, the same thing could be asked of the gods. Are they but a human convention serving the useful purpose of regulating society through fear of punishment and giving hope to us in difficult times, or are they natural beings?

"Very good, Euathlus. You have learned well the lessons I have given you. But let us now get back to the suit I have threatened you with."

I think such an action would be most unwise.

"How so?"

You, good Master, would be the one to suffer.

"I? On the contrary, Euathlus, I should be the winner no matter the outcome. For if you win, I get my fee, according to our agreement that you pay me upon winning your first case; and if you lose, I also get my fee, by virtue of my having won my suit against you in court."

It would seem so, at first glance, but a closer look shows how I must win in either case.

"Explain yourself."

If I win the case you have brought against me, then the court will have decided that I do not have to pay you the fee. On the other hand, if I lose the suit, then according to our agreement I will not yet have to pay you the fee I owe you, for I will still not have won a case.

"Well done, Euathlus! Do we have here an example of the student giving a lesson to the Master?"

By no means. I humbly claim only to have followed closely the very excellent training given to me by the foremost of philosophers.

"But how do you account for this complicated situation concerning my fee, Euathlus? Why does it seem equally certain to each of us that we cannot lose? Can you explain this to me?"

I'm not sure. I should like to give more thought to the matter.

"Well, then, I shall tell you. It appears that we cannot arrive at a solution here. There are two contracts involved in this situation: the one between us, which requires your payment of my fee on the occasion of your first victory at the court; and there is the one between the two of us, on the one hand, and the law, on the other, wherein your first victory releases you from any obligation to pay me. Thus, your victory brings about a contradiction. The same result, it seems, cannot satisfy both contracts.

"But never mind. My pretended suit against you was merely a test of your learning, and you have passed with great distinction. I am even tempted to withdraw my fee, for as you know I am in little need of the money, but I prefer to hold you to our bargain lest you fall short of the *arete* I have tried to inculcate in you. That is precisely what encompasses the most important of the lessons I have given to all my students."

I look forward to fulfilling the promise you have seen in me. You have certainly made me feel more confident of my first victory at the courts.

"I am glad to hear it. But now I must go, for I am off to keep an appointment. Farewell, Euathlus."

Farewell, Protagoras, best and wisest of men.

XIII
STING OF THE GADFLY

For I do nothing but go about persuading you all, old and young alike, to take thought neither for your body nor your wealth, but first and foremost for the greatest improvement of your soul.

SOCRATES

Prelude

Although he wrote nothing, belonged to no school, and claimed no special knowledge, he became the western world's most famous philosopher: Socrates – the very name embodies the image of the archetype, the bearded old sage wrapped in a shabby garment, wandering incessantly about the city of Athens questioning its citizens concerning the knowledge they falsely believe themselves to possess.

Socrates, son of Sophronicus the sculptor, was born in Athens in 470 BC. He continued the method of dialectic, or question-and-answer technique, of Zeno and Protagoras, but its mood became one of Socratic irony: he typically began an encounter by first claiming ignorance, and then proceeding to question his interlocutor, seeking definitions whose rejection created aporia, or perplexity, thus leading the interlocutor to realize that he did not really know what he thought he knew. At other times, Socrates used his method to draw out from someone knowledge he possessed but of which he had been previously unaware. In such a manner Socrates became, like his mother, a "midwife," but one who helped give birth to truth. Although he was dubious of claims to knowledge, his scepticism was tempered with a belief that only by rational inquiry can man approach truth. And the approach to truth is necessary, for, since no one sins knowingly, an understanding of how to live well can help to make one virtuous;

the acquiring of such knowledge is worthier of one's attention than are such things as mere wealth and fame. For Socrates, the ultimate end of all human striving is eudaimonia, *or happiness, specifically the happiness which comes from living virtuously.*

In being sentenced to die, Socrates became western philosophy's first martyr, though by no means its last.

STING OF THE GADFLY

Athens, 399 BC, at the Court of Justice
The final count is taking place. Socrates has already been found guilty by 281 votes to 220 votes; he now awaits the sentence of the Court. As there is no fixed penalty for Socrates' alleged crime, both the prosecution and the defence have been obliged to suggest suitable punishment. Meletus proposed death as the penalty; Socrates countered with what he feels he deserves for having decided long ago not to spend his life in comfort, but rather to go about the city trying to improve his fellow citizens. "What does such a man deserve," he asked, "who has neglected those things valued so much by other men – wealth, family, military and civic appointments, public oratory – in order to gain the leisure required to exhort others to concern themselves first and foremost with their soul?" His answer: free meals in the *prytaneum*, that round building in the *agora*, where the Athenians have seen fit to honour the winners at the Olympic Games and others deemed worthy. "This is what I truly deserve," he declared with perfect candour. And he added, "If you insist on a fine, then by all means fine me according to my ability to pay – say, one mina; yes, that would be just, although Plato, Crito, and several others have urged me to suggest a thirty minae fine, which they will guarantee. Well, then, I propose thirty minae, should you prefer a fine rather than free meals in the *prytaneum* as my punishment." This is how Socrates set forth his proposed punishment to the Court, much to the dismay of his closest friends, who immediately sensed the danger inherent in so honest an answer.

It was Meletus, a rich man, the hook-nosed one with the lanky hair and sparse beard, who, with the support of Dikon, an orator, and Anytus, a democratic politician well aware of Socrates' frequent criticisms of Athenian democracy, brought against Socrates the charges of impiety and of corrupting the youth of Athens. There are few among Socrates' friends who doubt that Anytus is the main force behind the charges, but, in any case, it is Meletus who is the spokesman. Of course, those who are well acquainted with Socrates understand the ridiculous nature of such charges, for they know how the appearance of this shabbily dressed, snub-nosed, paunchy, barefoot – many would even say ugly – philosopher belies his inner beauty. But they understand also how easily swayed are the unthinking masses.

✳

At this very moment Socrates is recounting to himself what he has already explained in detail to the Athenians assembled here today: how his close friend Chaerephon went to the oracle of Apollo at Delphi and how the god answered his question, "Is there anyone wiser than Socrates?" The priestess replied, "There is no one." Socrates recalls how he had been unable at first to comprehend the god's meaning, for he knew that he was not the least bit wise; and yet he knew also that the god could not lie.

It was thus that he set about seeking the god's true meaning. He did so by questioning, one by one, a considerable number of his fellow citizens who were reputed to possess great wisdom. In each case Socrates was able to show not only that such a man possessed no true wisdom, but that he was less wise even than those ordinary citizens with no reputation whatsoever for wisdom.

All of this aroused great indignation on the part of those questioned in such a fashion, as well as among bystanders who observed the proceedings. Nonetheless, Socrates was able to draw a conclusion after many such encounters with politicians, poets, and artisans: they, like he, really knew nothing worth knowing, but unlike him they *thought* they knew something worthwhile. Socrates at least knew that he possessed no knowledge of value at all, and it was this recognition alone which made him wiser than others. This, he concluded, was the god's meaning. And thus he was able to divine the task the god had set before him – to go about the *polis* as a sort of gadfly, stinging his fellow citizens into shame for caring about wealth and prestige while ignoring truth, wisdom, and the culturing of their souls.

Socrates continued to perform this commended service by questioning men throughout the *polis*, day by day, testing their beliefs, and ultimately showing them that they had far to go to achieve that *arete*, or excellence, which they had presumed to be already their possession. Those who thought they knew the meaning of, and could adequately define and explain, such difficult notions as justice, knowledge, and piety, for example, were relentlessly interrogated by Socrates until they became able to see clearly the folly of their own presumption, and to recognize their ignorance. Unlike Anaxagoras, Socrates has written nothing; and unlike the Sophists, the gadfly of Athens charges no fee for such learning as he imparts to others; he is merely obeying the god's command.

✳

Socrates' present ruminations are interrupted by the arrival of the Court's decision: *he is sentenced to die.* He takes the news in calmly, passively, his mind already having travelled to another recollection: that of how he has always called into question everything and placed it before the sober judgement of reason. What this amounts to in practical terms is that he has continually threatened the very customs of Athenian social and religious life. He knows that this has been too much for the most powerful segments of democratic Athenian society to bear (it has been five years now since the Spartan-imposed rule of the Thirty ended and democracy was restored at Athens); for who can tell where such questioning might lead, what changes might be called for should Socrates' perception of the lack of harmony between reason and worldly conduct become widespread! Yet, in a moment of sceptical self-doubt, he asks himself, "Have I been right in thinking that no one errs knowingly? Is knowledge sufficient to bring about the good?"

But now Socrates is roused by his friends to conscious awareness of the fate that awaits him. In the face of death, he takes one last opportunity to speak, not in order to save himself, but in order to enlighten those who have condemned him.

"Let me begin by saying to those of you who have voted for my death that it is a pity you did not wait a little time, for, as you can plainly see, I am already an old man quite close to my natural end. You would have gained somewhat by showing a bit of patience in this matter, for as surely as I stand here condemned by you to die, you will stand condemned by those who will now see the Athenian state as the instrument that put to death a wise man, Socrates. I tell you, it matters little that I am not really wise, for they will say this in any case. But let me ask you a couple of questions before I go, for you all know how I love to seek answers.

"First, why have I been convicted here today, and, furthermore, sentenced to death by a greater majority than that which found me guilty? Perhaps you think – or would like to think – that it is because I lacked the persuasive power of arguments that might have convinced you to acquit me. No, this is not the reason. What I lacked today was the kind of disgraceful impudence which might have impelled me, as it has so many others in previous trials, to beg for my life, to weep and wail, or to say things which I knew you wanted to hear, merely so as to escape punishment, or even to bring forward my family so as to garner your sympathy. But, no, I would prefer to die having spoken as I always do than to live by speaking as you would wish me to. Life, after all, is not worth the sacrifice of one's soul.

"But let me ask you something else – namely, whether there is anything harder to escape than death. Perhaps you think there is no such thing; after all, death is inevitable for everyone but the gods. Yet there is indeed something much harder to escape than one's mortality. I speak of the unrighteousness, the evil, that runs more swiftly even than death. Old as I am, I have naturally

been overtaken by death's swiftness; but you, my accusers
and condemners, though both cunning and quick, are already
overtaken by wickedness. Thus, I shall depart under penalty of
death while you leave this place today condemned by the truth to
evil-doing and injustice.

"Let me therefore prophesy, fellow Athenians — for it is in the
face of death that one possesses the greatest prophetic power
— that after my death an even greater punishment shall settle
upon you. This is not what you expected, for you thought that by
sentencing me to die you would free yourselves from the burden
of giving an account of your own lives. But you will find that
others, younger than myself, will be more severe with you than I
have; and you will surely be even more offended with them. You
have not learned that it is impossible to avoid the reproach of
others for your bad living by killing men; on the contrary, the
only honourable way is not to persecute and suppress others but
to culture yourselves so as to make yourselves good men.

"We still have a few moments before I leave to go to the place
where I must die; and so, let me remind you of how remarkable
is that which has happened to me on this day. As you know, I
have always been shown my path by a divine guide, my *daimon*, if
you prefer. In dubious circumstances, my guide has always turned
me back from that which might harm me; but today, as I left my
house, and when I came here to the Court, and when I spoke
to you the truth of my gadfly nature, I was never at any point
opposed by my guide. Why? Because it is obvious that what has
happened to me today is not an evil, but, on the contrary, a great
good. Yes, it must be so, for my guide would have opposed me
were it not so.

"We can say then that death, which is commonly thought of
as the greatest of evils, is perhaps a great good instead. For surely
death must be one of two things: either a state of nothingness
and complete unconsciousness, or, as some men believe, a change
and a migration of the soul to another place, from this world to
another one. And if the unconsciousness is like the sleep of one
who is undisturbed even by the slightest dream, then death will

surely be a positive gain. For if a man were to choose that night on which he had slept most soundly and compare it with all the other days and nights of his life, and then tell us how many other days and nights had been spent more pleasantly than this one, I say that such a man, even were he King of Persia, would find precious few. If death is like this, then it must be a great gain for anyone, for then eternity becomes as a single night.

"But what if death is a journey to another place, one where all those who have already died are present? Well, my fellow Athenians, try to imagine what could be better than this. Surely such a journey would be worth the taking, for it would both deliver one from the pretended judges of this world and lead one to the true arbiters who, it is said, pass judgement there – here I am speaking of Minos and Rhadamanthus and all such demigods as were righteous in their own lives. And think of those others whom one might meet and converse with there: Orpheus and Hesiod and Homer, for example. Why, if this be true I would be willing to die not merely once, but many times. In such another world might I meet also the heroes of old, many of whom suffered death through injustice, just as I do, and I think I should find some pleasure in comparing my own sufferings with theirs. But more than all of this is the great pleasure I would gain from continuing to question those who claim to possess true knowledge, whether it be such heroes as Odysseus or Sisyphus or any of numberless others. There, at least, one need not fear being put to death for striving to know and to make oneself and others better!

"Therefore, my judges, know this to be a truth most singular: *neither in life nor in death is it possible for evil to befall a good person.* Such a one will not be neglected by the gods; nor has today's verdict been an accident of chance. I can see that for me to die at this point is a good thing, and that is why my *daimon* never sought to guide me away from the course I have taken here. That is why I feel no anger toward my accusers or my condemners, for they have not – nor could they have – done me any harm. I do, however, blame them insofar as they did most surely set out to do me injury, though without just cause.

"In view of all this, I have a final request of you, accusers and condemners alike. When my own sons have grown up, I ask that you punish them, and trouble them in the manner I have troubled you, if they appear to care for riches more than for the *arete*, the excellence, that should be the proper goal of all men. If they pretend to be something when they are really nothing, then reprove them for not caring about what is really important. In doing this you will make certain that my sons receive the justice they deserve. That is all I ask of you with the last words you shall hear me speak.

"I see now that the time has arrived at which we shall leave this place. Hence, farewell to all. I go to die; you to live. Which of these is the better neither you nor I can tell. The god alone knows."

XIV
ATOMS AND THE VOID

The world consists of atoms and the void, and from these come all
things.

DEMOCRITUS OF ABDERA

Prelude

*Democritus was born in about 460 BC and died in 370 BC, or slightly later. He
rejected wealth and honour in favour of philosophy, earning from his contem-
poraries the nickname* Sophia, *or* Wisdom. *Although he outlived Socrates,
Democritus is often regarded as a Presocratic philosopher, and one of the
foremost in view of his breadth of knowledge and logical acuity, as well as the
revolutionary atomism which he learned from his teacher, Leucippus.*

Continuing the tradition of the Milesian physikoi, *the natural philosophers,
Democritus sought the* arche, *or principle, of the world. He took on from
Leucippus the problem of resolving Being and the nonexistence of void, on the
one hand, with plurality and change, on the other. He did so by recognizing
the existence of non-Being, or void, as a special kind of Being, within which
collisions and combinations of atoms generate and transform the objects of
the world. He was the first philosopher to stress the notion of* cause, *which
he identified with necessity: for him there are no random events in the universe;
everything is determined by what has gone before.*

*The degree to which Democritus rejected the senses as a valid means to
knowledge is uncertain. He did, however, place a limit on sense-perception by
recognizing that the senses never tell us directly about that which, alone, exists
independently of them: atoms and the void. His work provided a ground for*

materialism, determinism, and atheism in the ideological struggle against idealism, teleology – the belief that Nature exhibits purposefulness – and religion.

Although Democritus wrote on a wide range of subjects, only a few fragments of his works have survived, mostly ethical ones. His philosophy profoundly influenced Epicurus, who adopted both his atomism and his central ethical notion of tranquillity.

ATOMS AND THE VOID

Abdera, c. 370 BC

The old man is laughing again. Leucippus' most brilliant pupil is now approaching his ninetieth year, but is still as acute of sense and reason as ever. This thinker whom the citizens of Abdera affectionately call "the laughing philosopher" surely has as much right as anyone to find humour in the follies of mankind, for he has seen more of the earth and its strange peoples and customs than any other mortal.

Like many of his predecessors, Democritus is interested in everything: man, the cosmos – both its origin and its nature – animals, plants, physics, astronomy, religion, and morality. And like Thales of Miletus, he has taught that knowledge and wisdom are more important than money and worldly power.

I would rather discover a single cause than gain the entire kingdom of Persia.

Like Heraclitus and Anaxagoras, Democritus has sacrificed wealth to prove his point. As a young man he spent his hundred-talent inheritance travelling to Babylonia, Egypt, Ethiopia, Persia, India, and many other lands. He returned to Abdera not with material goods, but with more knowledge than anyone had ever possessed. His inheritance spent, he began his life-long devotion to philosophy.

The citizens of Abdera thought it strange that a man could spend a fortune travelling the earth only to return with nothing. It was not long before charges were brought against him for violating an ancient Thracian law forbidding the squandering of one's inheritance: Democritus was threatened with the loss of his right to burial in his native town. Rather than defending himself, he read to the judges his *Megas Diakosmos*, or *Great World-system*. So moved were they at his words that they awarded him one hundred talents to replenish his patrimony, and pledged to erect a bronze statue in his honour during his lifetime, as well as provide full burial expenses upon his death.

Democritus has now written over sixty works covering an astonishingly vast range of topics. Many who have read him say his style rivals that of Plato. But in spite of his present fame in Abdera, he made little impression on the Athenians when he first visited them as a young man in search of the philosophers.

I came to Athens, but no one had heard of me.

This did not disturb the equanimity of Democritus, for he has always shunned both fame and dialectic. Nor is solitude a stranger to him, for even as a young man he began to spend long periods alone in order to deepen his meditation on the world. Democritus has never founded a school such as the Academy, which Plato established some seventeen years ago. In fact, he is fully despised by the idealists for his godless materialism. Indeed, it is even said that Plato has wished to burn as many of Democritus' writings as he might lay hands on. Plato does not mention Democritus in his own works. Democritus does not care. It is not fame he wants, but to educate his fellow citizens.

Perhaps it is a good thing Democritus does not know that only a few fragments of his monumental work will survive him. Though he possesses great wisdom, he cannot foresee that he will become, for a very long time, a forgotten spirit in the chronicle of ancient philosophy. The world will wait two thousand years for the Englishman Francis Bacon to proclaim him the most profound of the philosophers of antiquity.

Democritus has taught many things about the universe and about man. He has continued Leucippus' teachings about the tiny atoms which make up the world; and he has taught his fellow citizens how to partake of the divine through conducting themselves rightly. On the constitution of the world, Democritus echoes his teacher's words:

There is nothing in existence but atoms and the void.

The *atoma*, or atoms, of Democritus and Leucippus cannot be seen by the naked eye and are indivisible: the very word *atoma* shows this, for it means "incapable of being cut or divided." Democritus says that matter is not infinitely divisible, as Anaxagoras said, for at the end of infinite division we would have nothing left; and, in any case, how can an infinity of nothings add up to the world we live in? Rather, matter is composed of indestructible bits of substance whose motion brings them together to make up the world in which we live. As for the origin, and infinite number, of atoms, Democritus tells us there is no need to account for the beginning of that which had no beginning, nor to account for the limit of that which is unlimited. In fact, the atoms share much of the essential nature of the Parmenidean One: they are ungenerated, unchanging, homogeneous, solid, indivisible, and eternal.

The specific properties of atoms depend on their form. It is the difference in their figure and size, as well as the way in which they combine, that accounts for the diversity of phenomena in the world. Even the human soul is composed of atoms – exceedingly small, fine, smooth, round atoms, like those of fire – diffused throughout the body.

The atoms move about in the void, or empty space, which, contrary to the claims of the Eleatic philosophers, does indeed exist. Void, or non-Being, is really a special kind of Being which makes possible the changes we witness everywhere about us. All things, except atoms themselves, contain a measure of void within themselves: thus, an apple is easier to cut through than a stone simply because it contains more void within itself.

We do not need gods or mythology to explain the diversity of the world, says Democritus: no Love and Strife, nor cosmic Mind – merely indestructible atoms and the void. The natural motion of atoms produces collisions which, when atoms are shaped in such a way as to be capable of interlocking, lead to combination, and hence the creation of various things in the world. Thus, objects form as atoms come together, and perish as atoms move apart. In this way have all things been created, including the planets. In fact, an infinity of worlds is constantly coming into and moving out of being through the random motions of these tiny particles, the downward movements of which create the *vortex* of necessity that brings them together.

Yet what is the principle which oversees the infinite motion of atoms? It is the law of attraction of like to like, Democritus tells us, that governs the formation of both inorganic bodies and all living creatures. Just as animals congregate together like unto like, and pebbles on the shore of the sea, so the atoms gather together, like recognizing like, to become the countless and multiform objects of our world.

It follows, according to Democritus, that our ability to sense the world is also dependent on the motions of atoms. Yet how is perception possible? Democritus has answered this question. We perceive things because they emit atomic *eidola*, "shells" or "films," which are copies of themselves and which act on our senses. This is how we are able to see the objects of the world around us. The atoms are similarly responsible for the perceptions of all other senses: colours are dependent on the degree of smoothness or roughness of *eidola*; sounds result when atoms cause vibrations of the air to strike our ears; it is similar with smells; tastes depend on the many different shapes of atoms; and this is also true of touch. All sensation, in one way or another, involves contact of atoms with each other. Even the mind itself works in such a way: how else could thought produce motion in a body!

Indeed, Democritus says that our own condition contributes greatly to our perceptions of things, just as the condition of all other animals tempers their perceptions. Thus, by convention we name sweetness, bitterness, redness, heat, and so on (knowing that what is sweet to one individual may not be so to another, nor even to the same person at different times). In reality, however, there are only atoms and the void. Were all life on the earth to die out, what would remain? *Not* colour, sweetness, redness, and all the other perceptible qualities, but only atoms and void; for sensual phenomena require sensing beings to *experience* them and then come to agreement on what qualities they possess.

Does this mean that those things we perceive are mere chimaeras? Not at all, says Democritus: they are the result of the movement of atoms in the void. This accounts for our very existence as sentient beings, as well as our ability, through the use of our senses and reason, to preserve our lives amid the atomic flow, and to judge and select wisely from among the various possible pleasures only those which truly enhance the harmony of our being.

Protagoras, in saying that "man is the measure of all things," went too far in calling every perception true, insists Democritus, for if this were so, then it would be true that *not* every impression is true. Why? Because this itself is also an impression and its truth shows the falsity of every impression's being true. Nonetheless, there is a measure of truth in our perceptions, even though it be a dark, obscure truth. But it is reason which has the power to give us what the senses do not – even though they open the way for reason to act – for through reason we gain genuine knowledge of the existence of atoms and void as the foundation of the world.

Democritus explains all things from atoms, even life itself. He says that life first began in warmth and moisture. Through many ages and long experience, humans learned how to forage for food, and through recognition of what is advantageous they began to live together in groups, articulate sounds into languages – first spoken, then written – weave clothing, cultivate the earth, repose in the warmth of the hearth, and learn the crafts that soften the harshness of daily life. And all this is of necessity, for every occurrence has its *cause*. Belief in chance is only ignorance of the causes which necessarily bring about all things. Yet necessity is also a great teacher, for it has led mankind to the laws which promote peaceful relations, and to all the conventions which make life in society possible.

Democritus admits that we cannot see the atoms of which he speaks, but he says we know they exist because our reason informs us that, in order to account for the world the way it is, we must recognize the eternal motions of atoms through space.

All this Democritus tells us. He has given much more, however, to the citizens of Abdera, as well as to the world, than a theory of how things have come to be as they are. He has taught men *how to live.* The goal of life, he says, is *ataraxia,* tranquillity. The well-being of the soul comes from a peaceful and moderate life unaffected by fear or passion or envy.

One must keep one's mind on what is attainable, and be content with what one has.

One might think that this leads men to mere sensual pleasure, but this is not so, for Democritus' serene pleasure is of the higher kind. And those who cultivate the love of wisdom, whose name is *philosophia,* will always be in control of pleasure.

One should choose not every pleasure but only those connected with what is good.

Democritus exhorts us to do good in our daily lives. Those who are generous, he says, will not seek a reward, for they will have freely chosen to do good. And he warns of the severest consequence of failure to live well.

To live badly is to spend a long time dying.

Most importantly, Democritus cautions that bringing harm to oneself is a thing most unfitting.

One must respect one's own opinion most, and this must become the iron law of one's soul, preventing one from doing anything improper.

It is not difficult, Democritus says, to bring good to oneself, rather than harm; and he advises others on those subjects pertaining to their well-being.

On happiness:

What is the road to eudaimonia, or happiness? The satisfaction of the proper needs of the body and mind. This can be accomplished easily, for the things which make life miserable are not unmet needs of body or soul, but rather an incorrect understanding of those basic needs.

On conducting one's daily life:

Live simply, here and now, for looking always to the future obliterates what is actually present. Here we have a spiritual exercise which leads one to serenity.

On wealth and poverty:
Greater desires create greater needs, and so the unlimited desire for wealth is more enslaving than extreme poverty.

On extravagance:
Shall we, then, never indulge ourselves? Yes, but let the occasion be always both rare and recognized as the luxury that it is.

On controlling anger and desire:
Mastery of passion is the mark of a superior mind.

On philosophy as therapy:
Just as medicine cures the body, so philosophy sweeps disturbing passions from the soul.

On parenting:
The greatest gift of a parent to children is the example of self-discipline and moderation.

On false piety:
It was strife in the heavens that first frightened humans into imagining gods as the causes of lightning, thunder, and eclipses; but these phenomena, too, are merely natural consequences of the interactions of atoms in the void. The wise person does not attribute to the gods powers which they do not possess.

On man's goal in life:
In the end, man's atoms disperse into the void; meanwhile, his telos, *or natural goal, is pleasure of the highest kind. Philosophy can help him to choose only such pleasures as do not bring pains in their wake.*

Democritus is an old man now, thinking back on a long life. The founders of worlds of thought were gone from this earth before he was born: Zarathustra, Buddha, Lao-Tzu, and Confucius have been dead for more than a century. So, too, has Pythagoras. And the Battle of Marathon has always been for Democritus a memory of events recounted by others. Yet his own time has also been one of great names and momentous events: Aeschylus, Sophocles, Euripides, and Aristophanes − masters of the stage; Herodotus, father of history; Hippocrates, founder of medicine, who pledged himself to the care of others; Pericles, who led Athens into its golden days; the glorious Parthenon, its creation a homage to Athena, divine patroness of the city; the tragic war of the Peloponnese; and Democritus' beloved teacher, Leucippus.

Then there was Socrates. It has been almost thirty years now since the gadfly of Athens drank the hemlock. Plato, who founded his Academy when he was about forty years old, is now fifty-seven. And two years have passed since the earthquake destroyed the temple at Delphi.

But in this time also lives the future, continuously being born and waiting to be born. At Stagira, in Thrace, the fourteen-year-old boy destined to become Plato's most gifted pupil ponders the night sky and the mysteries of the universe, wondering how it all began and whence it may lead; and while new and greater empires await their turn to rise and fall, Philip of Macedonia, the man who will be king, dreams of conquest and of the son who will overcome the world.

Yes, Democritus is an old man now – one who has seen more than most men imagine – but he is no fool.

Fools want to live long, because they fear death.

The old Master has lived a long life, and he is ready to face death without fear or false hope. The atoms of his body and soul will separate and go their way, drawn by the *vortex* of necessity, indestructible as time, and a few fragments of his towering works will glimmer in the darkness of worlds to come, reflecting in their glow the days that gave birth to the gentle laughter and serene contemplation of the materialist philosopher Democritus of Abdera.

XV
THE REPUBLIC

It is the philosophers who must become kings in our cities.

PLATO

Prelude

Plato, whose real name was Aristocles ("best and renowned"), was born into a wealthy aristocratic Athenian family in about 427 BC. As a young man, he was so deeply affected by the trial and execution of Socrates in 399 BC that he abandoned a planned political career and turned his attention to philosophy. Some twelve years later, after travelling to Syracuse and other cities, he opened a school, the Academy, on the outskirts of Athens; there he continued a lifelong dedication to the Socratic goal of seeking wisdom. The Academy remained a thriving centre of Platonism until it was closed almost nine hundred years later by the emperor Justinian in AD 529.

Plato's writings are the earliest complete philosophical works that have survived from ancient Greece. They are written in dialogue form, with Socrates as the central character, and are as famous for their stylistic elegance as for their philosophical brilliance. They expound various aspects of Platonism, within which the world of the senses provides but an impoverished and fleeting shadow of an imperceptible, real world of Forms *or* Ideas, *accessible only to the intellect. The world of sense is a world of opinion; the world of Forms is a world of knowledge.*

Through the Academy, Plato hoped to contribute to the establishment of a truly just state. His dialogue The Republic *examines the concept of justice*

*and the conditions for the establishment of a just society, and it considers in
detail the proper manner of education of its leaders, as well as the reasons why
they must be philosophers. It was through Plato that the word* philosophy
*first gained a wide currency, his writings imparting a distinct notion of what he
meant by it. Plato's influence on succeeding philosophy has been rivalled, among
the ancients, only by that of Aristotle.*

THE REPUBLIC

Athens, c. 360 BC

Although the Master is now sixty-seven years of age, his shoulders
are still almost as wide as when he was given the nickname "Plato,"
the broad-shouldered one, in his youth. The school he started
when he was forty, the Academy, is now twenty-seven years old
– almost exactly the same age as Plato was when his own Master,
Socrates, drank the hemlock. Today Plato is giving his students a
lesson from his well-known work *The Republic*. It is a lesson that
will take them far beyond the fleeting and imperfect world of
the senses to another world – strange at first encounter, until its
eternal perfection and permanence eventually yield to the power
of inquiring reason.

Among those present today is the young Stagirite, whose
name is Aristotle, and who is proving himself to be not only the
most inquisitive but also the most ardent and capable disciple at
the Academy. Plato has just now begun to speak of the subject he
introduced at the end of yesterday's lecture.

"Justice is our topic today," he announces, "and we shall
approach her heedfully, so as not to rush into a misapprehension
of her nature. We can best accomplish this, I think, by means of
a little allegory. Let us therefore imagine," he exhorts, "a group of
humans dwelling in an underground cave, the long entrance of
which leads gradually downward from the light of day. And let
us suppose that from early childhood these beings have lived in
the cave, their legs and necks chained so that they cannot move;

neither can they see anything beside or behind them, for their chains prevent such motions. They must look, then, only directly to the front, where a broad wall of the cave lies before them. Behind them, and a little above them, is a fire blazing brightly, and between the fire and the shackled humans is a raised walkway.

"Now, let us further imagine ourselves looking behind the prisoners. We see a low wall running along the raised walkway, much the same as the screen which marionette players have in front of them and over which they show their puppets. And along this walkway continuously pass many travellers carrying all manner of objects – statues of men and animals, tree-shaped carvings, urns and other containers, as well as a host of other commonplace things. Some of the travellers pass by silently, others with the sounds of speech or footsteps.

"This is a strange image, is it not?" asks the Master, who in return receives from his pupils a thoughtful, silent chorus of affirmative gestures. "Yet, what does it mean? Well, we shall see presently, but first let us complete the scene which I have begun to describe. Given the fire blazing behind the prisoners, and the parade of travellers passing along the walkway between the fire and the prisoners, it is clear that shadows of the travellers and of the objects they are carrying will be cast by the fire onto the wall in front of the prisoners. Furthermore, it is obvious that these shadows are the only things the prisoners will see, for let us remember that they cannot even look sideways in order to see each other.

"Well," continues Plato, digressing momentarily in order to sharpen the focus of his students, "at this point you may think these creatures quite alien to yourselves and the world with which you are familiar. Yet, we shall see that they are no different from us, for they see only their own shadows, or the shadows of their fellow prisoners, or those of the many travellers and their carryings, all of which are thrown onto the wall in front of them. And tell me this: were there to be echoes resounding in the cave from the vocal utterings or footsteps of those who pass along the walkway, would not the prisoners consider these sounds to be coming from the shadows cast onto the wall of the cave?"

"I see no other conclusion," offers a pupil.

"So," Plato continues, "let us now ask whether, if the prisoners were able to converse with each other, they would not suppose that what they were naming was actually the very things in front of their eyes." Here Plato looks directly at one of his students, indicating that he wishes him to attempt an answer.

"I believe that is exactly what we should suppose," the student responds, after carefully measuring his words. "They would name the shadows which have been cast onto the wall from the things you have described."

"Then would you also agree," asks Plato, "that when they uttered statements concerning these things, they would judge the truth or falsity of those statements in accordance with what they had seen — that is to say, in accordance with the nature of the shadows?"

"That seems correct," the student replies.

"You would agree, then," continues Plato, "that to the prisoners the truth concerns nothing other than the shadows of these things?"

"That would...seem to be the case," the student responds, hesitantly.

"Good. Now consider what would happen if, right at this very moment, we were suddenly to release a prisoner. Imagine him as we unshackle him. He stands up and stretches, turns his head and sees the walkway and the fire, and then begins to proceed along the walkway toward the light at the cave's opening. He glances around, but the glare begins to have an excessively powerful effect on his eyes, preventing him from seeing clearly the things of which he has always seen only the shadows. It is a painful experience, all in all, judging by the way he is squinting in order to protect his eyes. Yet, we must now imagine his extreme distress when, just as he reaches the cave's opening to the upper world, we tell him that everything he has seen before has been an illusion, and that for the first time, at precisely this moment, he is seeing that which really exists!"

The students are quite entranced as they struggle to apprehend the Master's every word while he continues his astonishing tale of the prisoner's journey into the light. "Imagine, if you can, our prisoner's response to such a revelation. Will he not rather believe that the dark shadows of his underground prison are more real than the glaring objects he now sees before him?"

"He must at first think so," volunteers a student.

"Yes, undoubtedly," adds another.

Plato continues, pleased by the apparent enthusiasm of his students. "Truly, he must first grow accustomed to the brightness and clarity of the upper world, must he not? For were we to bring him at once into the bright sunlight he would suffer pain and be unable to see clearly the world of objects he is now being told is real. Thus, he must move gradually from the easy perception of shadows to reflections of things in water, and finally to things themselves. Then he will look upon the heavens and see the moon and stars, whose light his eyes will tolerate much better than that of the noonday sun.

"Later, though, he will be able to see the sun and to contemplate and understand its power over seasons and weather, and its role as a veritable guardian and cause of many things in the world. And in such an enlightened condition he must be imagined to pity his fellow-prisoners in the cave, who, in self-delusion, believe that they live in a world of reality. Surely he would care nothing any longer for such honours as might be bestowed on a man in such a world. Would he not be willing to endure anything rather than return to think and live as his subterranean comrades continue to do?"

The students gesture in agreement, and Plato, convinced that he has successfully made his point, moves on. "Well, then, let us consider what would happen were he suddenly sent back to his shackles in his familiar position between two of his prisoner comrades. Suppose that he had to compete with them in making judgements about the shadows. Would he not fail utterly, his eyes now being wholly unaccustomed to the darkness of the cave? This being so, what would his fellow prisoners make of him? They would say, would they not, that he went up and came down and, as a result of his experience, is much the worse off. 'Let none dare to free any of us and send us up,' they would exclaim, 'lest we send him straight to Hades!'

"Perhaps we can now see the meaning of the allegory I have presented to you. First of all, what do you take to be the prison-house of the cave?"

"It is the world of sight, of the senses," offers a student, tentatively.

"Very good. And what of the light of the fire?"

"It must be the sun," enjoins another.

"Excellent!" Plato commends, before advancing to his crucial question. "Now what can we say of the freed prisoner's journey upward out of the cave?"

Plato waits, but at first none of his pupils is forthcoming. Then, calmly and deliberately, the young Stagirite, Aristotle, offers an explanation: "The prisoner's journey upward is like that very ascent of the soul into the world of the intellect, a world in which, with great effort, the idea of the Good may appear to the traveller. When once the traveller experiences the Good he knows it to be the source of Beauty and of Reason and Truth."

The Master is well pleased, though not the least surprised at his young acolyte's perceptive response. "Yes," Plato adds, "for where else but on such a world can those who would be rational fix their gaze? Let us not marvel, then, that our prisoner who has ascended to such heights becomes unwilling to descend once again to the cave, to the world of ordinary human affairs, for now his soul wishes to cleave to that upper world wherein eternal and changeless reality lies, and to remain there in its true home. For the perception of these things has made of our prisoner a *philosopher*.

"But what is a philosopher?" Plato asks, pausing before beginning to answer his own question. "It is one who, above all else, loves true knowledge and wisdom rather than mere opinion. Yet, as we have seen from our little allegory, the world of the shadows in the cave is the one in which society dwells, a world of the senses, of objects perpetually in a state of becoming. In such a world, the best one can gain is an *opinion* of those things which are always in a state of flux. The upper world to which our freed prisoner has ascended, on the other hand, is the world of true *knowledge*, reached not through the senses, but rather through the intellect. This is the world of the perfect Forms of things, in which the philosopher encounters and apprehends the Good, and also Justice, Truth, and Beauty, while the man of opinion, living entirely in the world of the senses, experiences only faint copies or shadows of these.

"And what are the Forms?" Plato continues, leading his pupils further into a new and wondrous realm. "They are what constitute the real world of eternal and changeless Being: I speak not only of those Forms such as Goodness, Justice, Truth, and Beauty, but also all the eternal Forms of the things whose shadows we see in our daily lives."

Here the Master gives an example in order to link the world of Forms to his pupils' everyday experience. "Take a table, for instance. However similar one table may be to other tables, a given table will also differ in some way from all other ones. Some are more clearly tables than others; we may wonder whether a particular table is not more properly to be called a bench or a desk; and so on. None is perfect, no matter how far we search over the earth. Each can be improved in some way, for it differs in some respects from the ideal or perfect table. Furthermore, each one is in a constant state of change, ebbing, however slowly and minutely, toward decay. Yet if we are to have true knowledge rather than mere opinion, there must be a perfect Table, eternal and unchanging, to which all these copies – or, we might prefer to say, shadows – approximate, and from which comes our recognition of all its various manifestations. This Form of the perfect table does not exist in the world of everyday life, however, where dwell only the shadows of things; no, it exists rather in the world of the intellect, to which reason alone has access. And so it is with all things whose shadows we glimpse in the world of the senses.

"One can see, then, how the true nature of the most important things – such as Goodness, Justice, Truth, and Beauty – are accessible only to the philosopher, while the ignorant crowd lives with opinions based on the shadows of these things, taking them to be the things themselves and therefore taking their opinions to be genuine knowledge. You may recall to memory – as I often do when I speak of such things – Socrates' fate at the hands of those who dwelt, utterly unaware, in the world of the shadows, not knowing anything but a faint semblance of perfect Justice, and yet empowered to distribute that of which they were ignorant unto even those such as the wise Athenian gadfly. In such a world of shadows those about us continue to dwell.

"Well, in any case, we have now reached the point where we may summarize the teachings of my allegory. It shows us how reality eludes us; how only the philosopher can perceive reality by virtue of elevated powers of reasoning; and it illustrates how most men do not believe the philosopher even when he tells them about reality – recall Heraclitus' complaint that even while present to his words, the Ephesians were absent and heard nothing.

"Look with pity, then, upon those who have seen the Good and who have seen Justice, and imagine them languishing in our everyday world, under compulsion to argue in the law court about the images or shadows of Justice, striving to interlocute with those who have never perceived absolute Justice, who have known only mere opinion about things. Now, would such a one who has known the world of the intellect be any more able to speak of true Justice to his countrymen than our freed prisoner would be to convince his fellow prisoners in the cave that they were seeing only a shadow of the real world, and that reality lay above them in another realm?"

"That is not at all likely," ventures a pupil.

"Well, then, we are agreed on this point. But as we were speaking yesterday of the manner of founding a truly just and flourishing city, in which all citizens might also flourish, we must now admit that my little allegory bears heavily on this matter. For it is clear that the rulers of such a city must of necessity be philosophers who, like our freed prisoner in the sunlight, have perceived with their intellect the world of Forms – since only those who are able to recognize Justice ought to be its dispensers. The allegory of the cave has shown us precisely this.

"Let us ask, then, what must be done if we are to create the ideal city, one whose perfect justness will last. It should be evident by now that this will happen only when the philosophers become kings in the city or, on the other hand, when those who are presently kings or potentates learn to seek wisdom as the philosophers do. Only in this way can political power and wisdom become one. If we cannot do this, we shall fail to avoid more of the same troubles that have beset, and continue to plague, our cities. Thus, a great part of our task in creating the just city lies in our cultivation of its proper class of rulers, namely the Guardians, or philosopher-kings, whose souls are alloyed with gold and who therefore will rule with perfect justice. The other classes are two in number: the Auxiliaries, whose souls contain silver and who will be perfectly suited to assist the Guardians in their imperative task, and to defend the *polis*, the city-state, against all threats; and the Producers, who by virtue of the iron in their souls, will be ideally fitted to supply by their labour the needs of all.

"When we go away from here today, let us think on these things. Tomorrow we shall continue our discussion by considering in detail the features of the perfectly just *polis*, whose Form rests in the upper world, accessible only to the intellect: a waiting pattern for mankind. And we shall examine the four cardinal virtues of the perfect city: *justice, wisdom, courage,* and *temperance*. We shall discover the ways in which social justice in such a city reflects the fact that each class works as it is properly fitted. And we shall also see that within an individual citizen, justice will be first and foremost a felicitous harmony of the three elements of the soul – that is, of *reason, courage,* and *desire* – with reason firmly in control as the overseer. In the Guardians, whose controlling principle is wisdom, the reasoning part of the soul will dominate; in the Auxiliaries, whose principle is courage, the spirited part; and in the Producers, desire. These dominating parts of the soul determine the highest pleasures of each class as well: in the Guardians that of reasoning; in the Auxiliaries that of victory or honour; in the Producers that of satisfaction of desires. Temperance, or self-discipline, however, must become a virtue common to all classes in the just state.

"We shall also consider the three principles concerning relations among classes, upon which the city is built and maintained. First, that of equal shares in the wealth of society; second, that of a proper limit to the size of the *polis*; third, the recognition of individual merit, no matter from which class a citizen comes. And we shall see how women, though physically weaker than men, are nonetheless capable of aspiring to the same things as men – even to guardianship of the city.

"Having already dealt in our earlier discussions with the weaknesses of the four inferior forms of *polis* – timocracy, or kingship; oligarchy, or the rule of wealth; democracy, the rule of the people; and tyranny, the rule of one strong man – we shall at last come to the idea of the perfect city-state, whose hallmark is Justice. We must imagine ourselves to be its creators; and must therefore seek with our intellect to comprehend its exact Form and the precise manner in which to manage the selection and education of the Guardians so as to ensure the best possible incarnation – not to mention the continued existence – of the just city. Only when we have accomplished this shall we be able to ask, with clear understanding, whether such a perfect city is really possible or whether our hopes concerning it are utterly in vain. But we shall wait until tomorrow to investigate this matter in greater detail."

Leading his disciples toward the outdoors, the Master exhorts them to philosophy with his closing words: "Always remember that of all things wisdom is greatest and closest to the divine, and that those whose true wealth is wisdom and virtue, rather than gold and silver, will ever look down upon the baseness of political ambition and material wealth. They will shun them as a plague worse than the one which laid Pericles and so many other Athenians to rest not so long ago, for they shall be those who have seen the Good. They shall be lovers of wisdom, *philosophers*."

XVI
ATHENS' ONE FREE MAN

I have come to Athens to alter the currency.

DIOGENES THE CYNIC

Prelude

Diogenes the Cynic was born late in the fifth century BC in Sinope, on the Black Sea. He was apparently exiled from his native city for his involvement in counterfeiting the currency, and he travelled to Athens, where he became a student of Antisthenes (c. 444-368 BC). Like a dog (the word cynic *comes from the Greek word for "dog"), Diogenes wandered the streets of Athens as a vagrant, living in a tub on the outskirts of the city and owning nothing. A street philosopher in the manner of Socrates, he opposed the artificiality of social conventions and extolled the virtue of studying Nature – not in order to explain things, but rather to learn how to live well. For Diogenes, ethics was the only true philosophy. He had nothing but disdain for the metaphysics of Zeno and Plato, in opposition to which he advocated, and lived, a life of simple independence, of* autarcheia, *or self-sufficiency.*

Two anecdotes suggest Diogenes' character. Late in life he travelled to Corinth, where he was captured by pirates and sold as a slave. Seeing Xeniades, he said, "Sell me to that man, for he needs a Master." Xeniades bought him and was so pleased with the way Diogenes tutored his children that he declared, "A good genius has come into my household." He soon gave Diogenes his freedom.

Also at Corinth, Alexander the Great, having heard of Diogenes' fame, sought him out. The great king came upon the philosopher sunning himself against a large rock, whereupon he greeted Diogenes and promptly offered him anything he desired. Without hesitation, the old man said, "Very well. Stand out of the way, for you are blocking the sun." Alexander is reported to have replied as he rode off, "If I were not Alexander, I should choose to be Diogenes!" It has also been said that, strangely, both men died on the same day in the year 323 BC.

ATHENS' ONE FREE MAN

Athens, c. 340 BC

Diogenes is again begging from a statue. He says it is training in the art of being denied. In exchange for an obol, he gives philosophy, but since the Golden Aphrodite refuses to give him anything, he withholds his wisdom. He mumbles something about her being the Athenian monument to lechery, and he moves on.

Diogenes acts in like manner with the citizens of Athens. For a small price he imparts a gem of wisdom. If he can teach a man nothing, neither will he accept payment. Yet Diogenes is not always so completely irreverent. Yesterday he made a sacrifice to the gods as a token of his gratitude. On his thumbnail he crushed a louse and promptly flicked it into the air, declaring, "Here, gods of Olympus, take back all that you have given me in life."

Diogenes prides himself, if on anything, on living simply. He resides in a large tub in the Metroum, the temple built almost a century ago in an attempt to appease the goddess Cybele and to free Athens from the great plague. He owns nothing and is therefore a slave to nothing. When once he saw a child drinking water from his hands, he threw away his cup, marvelling that one so young had outdone him in simplicity of living. Since then he has tried in every way to live a life devoid of luxury.

The Athenians recall how Diogenes' father, Hicesias, was disgraced for counterfeiting currency. When the citizens of Sinope condemned Diogenes to leave the town, he merely laughed and retorted, "And I condemn you to *remain* in Sinope!" Arriving in Athens, he declared, "I have come here to alter the currency." And he has lived up to his word, for he stands firmly against all those conventions by which the lives of the unquestioning masses are guided.

For Diogenes, philosophy is no mere abstract exercise – it is his very life, and it is here on the streets and in the porticoes of Athens that he daily reveals both. It is here that he wanders about – just as Socrates used to do – engaging in disputation with old and young alike, challenging with his razor wit and logic the received beliefs of convention, and proving himself always too strong for any opponent.

His encounters have already become legendary, and anyone who follows him on his daily peregrinations will bear witness to his ability to defend himself against all manner of attack. Today he has encountered a group of young men who, one by one, are challenging the old Master, who rebuts them at every turn.

✻

Old men such as you, Diogenes, are a threat to the very order of our city-state. It would be better for us if you left Athens and returned to your native city.

"I am no enemy of the Athenian state; rather, I am its salvation. The real enemy is convention, the set of rules followed mindlessly by young fools such as yourself, including the false piety, the chasing after honours, the unthinking quest for wealth, and the expectation of luxurious living – as if happiness had anything whatever to do with these things."

You are no philosopher, just an ignorant man trying to become wise.

"You are perceptive enough to see what I am, but not judicious enough to name it correctly. Nonetheless, although contradicting yourself, you have described precisely what a philosopher is!"

Do you know how many they are who laugh at you, Diogenes?

"Many are the unknowing fools who, completely mastered by convention, laugh at those who dare to live by Nature's dictates – and yet, in spite of this, I do not feel laughed at by any of them."

You had little loyalty to your native city of Sinope, and you appear to have none to your adoptive city-state of Athens. How do you defend yourself against such a charge?

"In my lifetime I have seen the decline of the *polis*, and the various attempts to bring and hold the Hellenes together under a single leadership, be it Spartan, Theban, or Macedonian. Presently we can discern the prospect of a Greek world ruled by Philip of Macedonia. Indeed, it now looks as though war between Athens and Philip is imminent and − who can say with certainty? − that the Macedonians may prove strong enough to take control of all the Hellenes. And don't forget that Persia still holds the Greek colonies of Ionia. You speak of allegiance to Athens, my young friend, but you do not see that such allegiance − not to mention that between man and man − however strong it remains, has already been eroded by the events that have occurred during my long life. As for me, such allegiance to one city-state, and consequent enmity toward another, is merely a further example of artifice. Nature has shown me that the world, the *cosmos*, is my *polis*. Hence, call me a *cosmopolitan* if you wish, for I am a citizen of the world; that is the only loyalty I wish to profess."

You ridicule the rich, but where would we be without them?

"We would be without poverty and hunger, two of the greatest evils plaguing mankind, and, what is more, we would be without slavery. A rich man is a disgrace, for his wealth is a measure of the impoverishment of others. Truly, I tell you that in the house of a rich man there is only one place to spit − in his face. It is the rich who are the biggest thieves of all, and yet the richer they become, the more ruthlessly they wish to punish little thieves."

You mock convention, Diogenes, yet you have nothing to place in its stead.

"On the contrary, had you listened to me in the past you would know that I have always declared a modest and virtuous life to be the only path to lasting contentment. This is what Nature teaches us. Conventional desires, such as those for wealth or position, serve only to destroy peace of mind. Virtue is its own reward and, being independent of the gods, is attainable by all. And what is virtue, you may ask. Eating simply, possessing nothing, desiring little, harming none, and defending oneself against opponents always with honesty. Honest poverty is better than the greatest wealth, to which one can only become a slave."

Urinating in public, housed in a tub, insensitive to the feelings of others: surely these are not the marks of a true philosopher!

"My actions are a mirror into my philosophy. If you gaze into that mirror you may yet see the folly of your unthinking devotion to meaningless convention. It is true that I lack the kind of politeness which serves generally as a shield to hide true feeling and opinion, but this is merely to say that I lack yet another artifice. Of what use is a philosopher who is afraid of hurting someone's feelings by what he says? It is important that people learn the truth and live their lives accordingly. If I shock you, let your disturbance be a pathway leading toward a virtuous life."

You, an old man dressed in rags, have dared to criticize Zeno and Socrates and Plato?

"Zeno could not have given his lecture at Athens had he not travelled here – yet he denied the existence of motion. Do you deny that you moved your lips in order to ask me your question?

"As for Socrates, who said, 'Know thyself,' I say that this is a fine sentiment, but let us go further and say, 'Master thyself,' for this alone – *autarcheia*, or self-sufficiency – is the way to happiness and the profoundest peace of mind.

"And what are we to say of Plato, who defines Man – and here he means a Form or Idea independent of all flesh and blood humans such as you and I – as a 'featherless biped.' Well, the crowd thought it rather humorous when I held aloft a plucked chicken and declared, 'Here, have a close look at Plato's Man!' I tell you that it is in the practical world – and for the most part in misery and squalor of one sort or another – that we mortals live. This, rather than some mystical realm of Forms, is the only world we can know.

"I give thanks to Socrates' pupil – my teacher, Antisthenes – who has done me the greatest favour by turning me into an exiled beggar. I am one who is dressed in rags and owns nothing, and I am therefore independent and contented. To this extent I am wiser than those who fall down before the preposterous conventions of society."

It seems to me that you denounce happiness because you are unhappy yourself! Perhaps this is also why you detest man.

"Like the Ephesians who could not comprehend a word of Heraclitus, you misunderstand everything. I have said often enough that happiness is the very goal of life for man – his *telos*. Yet we must ask *how* this goal is to be attained; this is precisely the problem. You think, perhaps, that pleasures of the flesh, or wealth, or honour will bring happiness. But these are the artifices of an unhappy city-state; together they constitute a force leading men *away* from happiness. I take pleasure in despising such pleasures. Nature shows us what our true needs are: a modicum of food, moderate toil, adequate shelter. Friends – so long as one maintains one's independence – also have a part to play, for sensible friends can always prevent a man from acting imprudently.

"Do not be fooled into thinking that pleasure will bring happiness, for it generally causes more trouble than it is worth. Happiness comes from a simple, natural, virtuous life based on *autarcheia*, or self-sufficiency, the greatest freedom and the only one that can never be taken away from anyone. Therefore, to own nothing is a good first step toward the *eudaimon*, or flourishing, life; for it is only by renouncing the world that we can gain it.

"As for men, I do not hate them, as you claim. On the contrary, I understand their weaknesses better than they themselves do. When I see the astronomer or philosopher at work, I regard man as the noblest of creatures, but when I see the interpreters of dreams and other charlatans, or the behaviour of the arrogant rich at table or in the *agora* or at the law court, I see no animal as ridiculous."

If you dislike the world of convention so much, old man, why not drink hemlock as Socrates did. By your philosophy one should think it an evil merely to live.

"Plato once called me 'a Socrates gone mad'; I think myself to be, rather, a Socrates become more consistent. It was unwise of Socrates to drink the hemlock, yielding thereby to convention and, though already old, throwing away years of philosophy and dialectic. He stated at his trial that he would have refused to give up philosophy even had the law court ordered him to do so; but he was willing to give up his life – even though his philosophy and his life were one and the same!

"Unlike Socrates, I refuse to be enslaved by unfair laws or ridiculous conventions. I have just told you it is man's folly I despise, not mankind. Why else am I here today talking to you and hoping to lead you away from convention and thereby change your attitude to your own soul, for you are like the musician who takes utmost care tuning his instrument while at the same time leaving his soul in utter discord.

"And hear this, my young friend: it is never an evil to live unless one leads a worthless life."

You are an impious man, Diogenes. You have little respect for our gods.

"Conventional piety is false piety. Do you think the gods as big fools as men – for this is how men portray them. Who but fools would then worship such creations? True piety, on the contrary, consists in listening to Nature and following her guidance."

Do you recognize beauty? I so often hear you rant against the ugliness of the world that I doubt it.

"I have often spoken of that which is most beautiful. Honesty is the thing of greatest beauty in the world. Have you not seen me going about Athens, as I often do in broad daylight, holding aloft a lantern as I look into the faces of those whom I meet, searching for an honest man? My lack of success in this regard is a natural consequence of the preposterous conventions which turn men away from honesty. For we live in a society that creates liars who, in order to succeed, must adopt the most repugnant artifices. Rare, indeed, is the honest man who will recognize the truth and live by it even though it cost him all the material comforts and honours reserved for the rich."

You claim independence, Diogenes, and yet you rely on our gratuities for your livelihood.

"I teach you, young pups, the folly of your words and actions, and point the way to your personal salvation. Surely that is worth something – if not more than anything you might purchase in the *agora*. If I had failed to teach you anything, I would likewise refuse your offering. I believe, however, that our present encounter has proven fruitful and that you may leave here with more sense than you came with."

I am one who truly wishes to improve himself, Diogenes. But how shall I start?

"Begin by trying always to act honourably and justly in defending yourself against those who are without honour or a sense of justice, lest you allow yourself to descend to their level. Live simply and humbly, accepting those limits which Nature herself has decreed for our kind."

You decry the present condition of society. How, then, would your world differ from our present state?

"We would lead a life of *philosophia*, a love of wisdom, based on self-sufficiency. This means a simple life for all, without property and yet without poverty and hunger, without laws favouring the rich – for there would be no rich – without slavery, and with the guiding hand of natural virtue directing all. Only in such a life would men and women find, at last, that security for which they have always longed."

✳

Sensing that they have gained from their encounter with Diogenes, several of the youths pass small sums of money to the old philosopher. Satisfied that he has succeeded in teaching them something useful, Diogenes accepts their offering. He thanks them before continuing to wander the streets and porticoes of Athens, not knowing whom he will meet next, remaining ready, as always, to instruct those who mistakenly believe that the way of artifice and the good life are one and the same.

XVII
MASTER OF THOSE
WHO KNOW

Man by nature desires to know.

ARISTOTLE

Prelude

Aristotle, Plato's most brilliant pupil, and perhaps the most influential philosopher in history, was born at Stagira, Thrace in 384 BC. His father, Nichomachus, was court physician to King Philip of Macedonia, and in 343 BC Aristotle was summoned by Philip to tutor his thirteen-year-old son, who was destined to become Alexander the Great. Believing that "man by nature desires to know" and that "the activity of the mind is life," Aristotle eventually acquired a learning that was truly encyclopaedic, and he wrote on a wider variety of subjects than anyone before him had done. He was the first thinker to attempt to classify all knowledge, developing theories in many areas, among which were the theory of the syllogism, which he considered the basis of logical argument, and detailed theories of language, metaphysics, ethics, politics, and art. He also wrote on mathematics, physics, biology, meteorology, psychology, and rhetoric, among other subjects. What we possess of Aristotle's works consists mainly of extensive lecture notes in a rough style that indicates they were probably never intended for publication. His style in published works, however, was highly praised by ancient critics for its elegance.

But Aristotle was not merely a theorizer, for in him the thinker and doer were united: he was as much a scientist as a philosopher. On leaving Plato's Academy, he carried out research in marine biology at Lesbos. Later, at his own school, the Lyceum, founded at Athens in 335 BC, he lectured and conducted, along with his students, comparative studies of political constitutions and in-depth studies and classification of hundreds of species of plants and animals.

After the death of Alexander in 323 BC, the Athenians rose up against Macedonia, and a charge of impiety loomed over Aristotle's head because of his past association with the monarch. In order to prevent the Athenian state from "sinning twice against philosophy" – the first sin having been the execution of Socrates – Aristotle fled to his mother's home at Chalcis, on the island of Euboea. There he died in the following year.

MASTER OF THOSE WHO KNOW

Athens, c. 330 BC

It is morning, the time when Aristotle usually lectures to his pupils at the Lyceum, which for five years now has been both gymnasium and sanctuary to those who wish to know. In the evenings he lectures to the citizens of Athens.

As the Master talks, he walks. His long, thin legs, fashionably short hair, and ring-laden fingers create a memorable impression for his young disciples. It is his habit of walking while lecturing that has given rise to the name *Peripatetic* for his school of philosophy, which differs from that of his own beloved teacher, Plato. Like Plato, though, Aristotle believes in reason and he uses it to construct detailed arguments concerning every subject his mind touches. It is not easy, at first, for his pupils to follow all the threads of his logic, but with perseverance they gradually become able to fathom his thinking and to gain in that kind of understanding which is relevant to everyday life.

Presently Aristotle is talking about practical philosophy.

"As the activity of the mind is life, and as we are interested in life, let us proceed to examine a question of central importance to the activity of the mind. Why do we say that 'the good' is 'that at which all things aim'? Plainly it is because every art, every pursuit, every inquiry is commonly believed to aim at some good. Well, as there are many different ends, let us see where consideration of them leads. The end of the medical art, for example, is health, whereas the end of shipbuilding is a seaworthy vessel. The end of economics, on the other hand, is a proper creation and distribution of wealth.

"But we must ask ourselves whether or not there is an end which we desire for *its own* sake, all other ends being for its sake – and, of course, we must assume that not everything exists for the sake of something else, for in such a case we would confront an impossible infinite progression. So, if there is such an end of the many things we do, would it not be prudent to attempt to discover its nature, since knowledge of it must surely be of great importance for our lives?

"Well, of all things that come to mind it is politics that seems to be most relevant to our inquiry. It is politics that determines what should be learned by the various classes of citizens within a *polis*, and it is politics under which fall the most highly regarded sciences and capacities of society: strategy, economics, and rhetoric, for example. The end of politics must therefore be – since it includes the ends of these other sciences and capacities – one which exists for mankind's good. And, further, it seems that it is a finer thing, and more akin to the divine, that this ultimate end be sought and attained not merely for a single man, but for the state as a whole. Such is the end, therefore, which constitutes the focus of our inquiry.

"What, then, is that *highest* good at which politics and, therefore, all our knowledge and pursuits aim? What, in other words, is the *greatest* good attainable through human action? In a word, it is *eudaimonia*, or happiness – a flourishing life, we might say – that general agreement proclaims as the good. Yet, among the many accounts given by the common man, as well as by men of wisdom, what is *eudaimonia* taken to be? Well, pleasure, wealth, and honour have all been put forth as answers to this question. And there are those who consider it a relative matter, such that health becomes happiness when one is recovering from illness, or wealth when one has sunk into poverty.

"But here let me remind you that much as we honour our friends, we must, according to the dictates of piety, honour truth even more. We will dispense, therefore, with detailed discussion of Plato's theory of Forms, or Ideas: I have often enough demonstrated to you its shortcomings. Suffice it to say here that what we are seeking is not something which is called 'good' through its resemblance to a single Idea – that is, a resemblance to that Form known as the Good, as Plato would have it – but rather something specific to, and attainable by, man. I hope I have made it clear in previous discussions that the Forms are not helpful in understanding the movement and change we witness daily in the world about us. Yet we must understand such movement and change if we are to recognize and attempt to attain a flourishing life.

"Very well, then. Let our question be thus: *How is it possible to live a* eudaimon, *or flourishing, life?*

"In view of the diversity of conceptions of happiness, perhaps we need first to determine more clearly the *ergon*, or function, of man, for just as a carpenter and a tanner have specific functions, so does man *qua* man have a function peculiarly his own. But it is not mere nutrition and growth, evidently, for these seem common to plants as well as to all animals. Nor is it a life of perception, for this faculty is shared by animals. There remains but one aspect of life and it is that which proves to be the essential characteristic of man – the life of the rational element, of reason, which means nothing other than an activity of the soul in accord with a rational principle. And since we are speaking of a good life, we must add that this is an activity in accordance with *arete*, or excellence, which we may also call 'virtue.' We might even say, more properly, that the essential characteristic of man is *activity in accordance with the best and most complete virtue in a complete life*.

"Thus, human good, happiness – the *eudaimon*, or flourishing, life – turns out to be an activity of the specifically human, rational soul in accordance with virtue. Well, then, let us proceed to consider what we must at this point: namely, both the relation of external goods to such happiness, and the general nature of virtue.

"Now, with respect to the former, we may note that such benefits as friends, wealth, and political power may be useful in the performance of noble actions. Further, it is also clear that a lack of certain things may deprive happiness of its lustre: things such as good birth, good children, and beauty, for example. Happiness, therefore, has a degree of dependence on external goods, about which I shall say more later.

"But let us now remind ourselves, from previous discussions, of the nature of *arete*, or virtue, for in doing so we may come to understand happiness more fully, just as the serious student of politics surely must if he is to attempt to improve men – which is to say make them more virtuous – through the best organization of the state.

"Recall, therefore, that virtue is of two kinds: *intellectual* and *moral*. Philosophical, or theoretical, wisdom belongs to the former, as does *phronesis*, or practical wisdom. Temperance and liberality, however, which are expressions of a man's character, belong to the latter. The origin and growth of intellectual virtue – of philosophical and practical wisdom – depend greatly on *instruction*. Moral virtue, on the other hand, is a result of *habit*: that is, we become just men by practising just actions, brave men by practising brave acts, temperate men by exercising temperance, and so on.

"You will remember from our last lecture the specific nature of moral virtue and so I shall not go into all the details again, but rather I shall remind you that moral virtue is a *state of character* of a particular kind – one which is concerned with choice of action. Yet what actions are chosen when one seeks to live virtuously? In a word, those which are a *mean*, relative to man, between two extremes each of which represents a vice, one being a vice of excess, the other a vice of defect.

"Notice that I have said the mean *relative to man*. By this I am suggesting a mean course of action between two extremes, determined by the choice of a man of practical wisdom who is therefore able to reason correctly about ethical matters. This mean, unlike a strict arithmetical mean, will not be the same for everyone, but rather it will be what is appropriate for the life of each. Just as one man may require more food than another, so will one man take more exercise than another, though each man in both instances be in accord with a mean relative to himself.

"To clarify this, let us look at some of the main forms of moral virtue. Courage, for example, is a virtue concerned with feelings of fear and confidence. The man whose confidence is excessive, such that he may needlessly place himself in danger, is said to be rash. The man who lacks confidence and exceeds in fear, on the other hand, is called a coward. The man of courage, who chooses the golden mean between extremes – though he be virtuous and happy in life, valuing it greatly and suffering anguish at the thought of death – nonetheless faces whatever dangers his practical wisdom deems necessary for a virtuous life.

"It is likewise with the other moral virtues. With respect to pleasure and pain, the excess is self-indulgence and the defect insensibility. The mean sought by the virtuous man is temperance. And when we consider the giving and taking of money, we recognize excess as prodigality – exceeding in giving, falling short in taking – and deficiency as meanness, an excess in taking and a falling short in giving. The mean is liberality.

"With respect to honour and dishonour, the mean might be called a proper pride, situated between the excessive vice of empty vanity and the defective vice of undue humility. Of the truth about things, we may say that the mean of truth-telling is the virtue, whereas boastfulness and mock modesty are, respectively, the excessive and deficient vices. And, of course, there is the righteous indignation which lies as a golden mean between the vices of envy and spite.

"Now, let us not forget that all of this choosing of virtuous actions – that is, of the mean – assumes a certain voluntariness and awareness of circumstances on the part of the chooser, as well as the power to carry out the actions in question. If a man is acting under compulsion, for example, in which case the cause exists in external circumstances, he can be neither praised nor blamed for his actions, since he is not part of the cause of them. But when awareness and deliberation precede a voluntary choice, then the resulting action becomes praiseworthy or blameworthy insofar as it is or is not carried out in accord with virtue.

"Thus, as I hope I have made clear, moral virtue is a habit of acting in a certain manner and is dependent on practical wisdom. The man who possesses practical wisdom always chooses the mean, pushing aside irrational emotions, choosing virtue in order to prepare himself for *eudaimonia*, the profound happiness of the contemplative life. Practical wisdom guides a man toward virtue because it utilizes intuitive reason; this, along with scientific knowledge, is the essence of that philosophical wisdom which longs to be directed toward the highest objects in a manner that completes it. In a similar manner, philosophical wisdom also depends on the continued use of practical wisdom in seeking out a life of virtue. Thus, we can say that it is no more possible to be morally virtuous without practical wisdom than it is to have practical wisdom without moral virtue

"Well, then, clearly we must now ask what are some of those things, other than philosophical and practical wisdom, which are able to help us to achieve the virtue which constitutes the gateway to happiness, to the flourishing life, which, as we have seen, is the end for which all other ends exist. Having already mentioned external goods and their relation to happiness, let us continue with that line of thinking and ask what role nature plays in a man's goodness. Here we can say for a start that within some fortunate men there are divine causes present which provide a virtue-loving character – a kinship, as it were, to virtue. But if one has not been reared under the right laws, then a proper training to virtue from an early age will be lacking. It would be better that men – since living temperately is not a pleasant thing for the young – had their nurturing, and even their occupations, fixed by law. In such a manner they would grow and become oriented toward a virtuous life. This is an important question concerning politics, and I will say more about it in a moment; but let us first consider another external good: friendship.

"That there is great value in friendship I have said many times.

Who would choose to live – no matter how many other goods he possessed – without friends? They are a veritable bulwark against misfortune, being a sort of refuge in such times, as well as a guardian of prosperity, which is always at risk. And on whose behalf is it better to exercise beneficence than that of friends. We can easily recognize that friendship is a boon to those of all ages. It helps the young toward virtue by keeping them from error. Those in the prime of life it leads toward noble actions, for friends help a man to think rightly. And as for old age, when one's abilities begin to fail, it is friends who take up the slack, as it were, and help to keep one on a right path. True friends have no need of justice, and it is generally believed a good thing to have many friends and that the same men are both good and friends.

"Yet to be a friend to others and to have friends, one must first possess something else: a proper love of self. Now, only the virtuous man will possess this, for he will find existence to be a good thing and will wish himself always that which is good, storing up memories of good acts and good relations with others, both as a reminder of how one should behave and as matter for contemplation. This love of self, then, which one ought never to confuse with mere vanity, exists insofar as, and because, one is good.

"Now, as I told you I would return to the topic of politics, let us begin by recognizing that man is a political, as well as a rational, animal and that only in a state with right laws will the excellence of men be the rule rather than the exception. It is in this sense that ethics becomes possible through politics, for the proper function of the state is to enable men to live flourishing lives and therefore to enable the state itself to become a flourishing one. Thus we can see clearly the main task of legislators – to create precisely that kind of state which leads men to virtue.

"But the same legislators will be aware that while most men rather obey necessity than argument, and punishment rather than what is noble, the good man, fixing his gaze on what is noble, will be moved by argument. The former, then, require that compulsive force of law based on practical wisdom, rather than argument, if they are to be good; and as it is particularly the young who are unable to judge wisely until they are instructed appropriately, allowance must be made for their early training as a means of forming the habit of acting virtuously.

"In all the higher things men do they imitate the gods, their supreme models of *arete*, of virtue. The best life for man, therefore, is one in accord with the highest virtue, which is *contemplative*. Such virtue is reason's highest activity, just as its objects are the best of knowable objects. Furthermore, contemplation is the most continuous activity, for we can contemplate truth more continuously than anything else. And the pleasure associated with the contemplation of truth is the greatest of pleasures, both in its purity and in its duration. Therefore, we can say with confidence that the pleasure of those who know and contemplate the truth is greater than that of those who merely inquire after the truth.

"And now we are able to see clearly that the man who has become virtuous through adhering always to the golden mean has already prepared himself for the contemplative life. So let us not think any longer of mere human things, of mortal things, but rather let us, insofar as it is possible and insofar as reason is divine, become immortal ourselves by striving to live in accordance with that divine reason which constitutes the very best of all that is within us. For we have seen that whatever is proper to a thing is by nature the best and pleasantest for it; and for man it is reason, even more than virtue, which makes possible the best and most pleasant existence. As for the one who leads such a life, though he may need a certain amount of external goods and takes the greatest pleasure in friendship, yet he is also the most capable of that *autarcheia*, or self-sufficiency, which Diogenes and others so often lauded precisely because it imitates that of the gods.

"Well, then, let us walk in the warm air in silence for a time, thinking all the while carefully on these things. Later we shall consider questions of every sort in order to ensure that what I have said about virtue and the contemplative life stands against the force of your logic."

✳

Thus has Aristotle described the man who approaches the pinnacle of moral virtue, the divine reason within him reaching its highest expression through the intellectual virtues of philosophical and practical wisdom. It is a general description, and yet it applies most perfectly to Aristotle himself, the Master of those who know, for he is one who has long followed the path of *theoria*, of contemplation of the highest truths. Such an existence, though beyond the everyday manner of being in the world, ever awaits those whose *arete* has prepared them to imitate divine blessedness. It is a life whose name is *philosophia*, the love of wisdom.

XVIII
SIX VIEWS OF A SCEPTIC

Every argument can be opposed by an equal argument.

PYRRHO OF ELIS

Prelude

Pyrrho, the acknowledged founder of Scepticism, was born around 365 BC and died in about 270 BC. He gave lectures in philosophy, travelled about the countryside, and lived a simple, tranquil life of poverty. Among his predecessors were Xenophanes, who said that even should a man encounter the truth he would not know it to be such, and Protagoras, who taught pupils to argue equally from both sides of an issue. For Pyrrho and for Pyrrhonian sceptics in general, philosophy was considered a practical art whose aim is detachment and ataraxia, or tranquillity. Yet one can attain tranquillity only through abandonment of the doomed search for truth — doomed because both sense-perception and reason are flawed and therefore uncertain at best.

Although he left no writings, Pyrrho is known to us through his disciple Timon of Phlius and, even more so, through Sextus Empiricus (fl. AD 200), whose Outlines of Pyrrhonism *gives an exposition of Pyrrho's thought, as well as comparing it with the Academic Scepticism that increasingly came to dominate Plato's school from about 275 BC. Pyrrho saw all conclusions as indefensible, and certainty as unattainable. He argued that the prudent person will suspend judgement and opt for tranquillity rather than truth. And since no theory can be trusted, one ought to accommodate oneself to the existing habits and customs of society, in order to be serene at all times. Whereas the Academic*

Sceptics developed sophisticated theoretical arguments against dogmatism, particularly that of the Stoics – including a collection of tropes, or modes of justifying suspension of judgement – Pyrrho's influence lay largely in his way of life.

SIX VIEWS OF A SCEPTIC

Elis, c. 290 BC

The Man

A painter by trade, Pyrrho has long since given up that activity in exchange for philosophy. He is a *skeptikos*, or sceptic, an "inquirer" into the grounds for the philosophers' statements concerning the truth or falsity and the goodness or badness of things. There are still many here in Elis who remember well the journey of young Pyrrho, son of Pleistarchus, to India with his teacher, Anaxarchus, and Alexander the Great. But that was a long time ago. Nonetheless, there are some who insist that it was among the sages – the Gymnosophists, or "naked philosophers" – of that eastern land that Pyrrho learned the heart of his philosophy.

Like Socrates and Diogenes, Pyrrho is a logical and highly-skilled interlocutor; and like them he has written no books. Yet many are drawn to him and to his simple, unpretentious manner of being. He lives with his sister Philista, a midwife, and he takes pigs and chickens to market and performs household duties impassively. Whatever vicissitudes Pyrrho encounters are faced by him indifferently. He accords no particular significance to meeting one person as opposed to another, nor to being in any given place at a given time. He maintains always a tranquil aspect.

And yet Pyrrho's actions are frequently unpredictable. At certain times he seeks the solitude he greatly cherishes; at other times he picks up and sets out on foot alone, telling none of his acquaintances, but inviting along with him some of those he meets along the way toward his destination – if, indeed, he has a destination at all. It has also been said that he once continued to speak for quite some time even after his audience had left. And another time, when Anaxarchus fell into a swamp, Pyrrho saw immediately that his teacher was in no serious danger, and so he continued walking and did not stop to help him. Some criticized him for this, but Anaxarchus later praised him for his admirable indifference and calmness. The esteem in which he is held by his fellow citizens at Elis became evident when they made him a high priest and, in his honour, exempted philosophers from taxation.

The Goal

Pyrrho has reasoned out the *telos*, or goal, of mankind: it is *eudaimonia*, or happiness. And he has found that which leads directly to the goal. It is not pleasure – though Pyrrho affirms that pleasure can often contribute to a flourishing life, or be a consequence of such a life. Nor is it merely the use of man's rational faculty, even though reason is essential to justifying one's choice of that necessarily unorthodox life which alone brings happiness. What leads directly to man's *telos*, says Pyrrho, is the same as that which best characterizes the gods: *ataraxia*, or tranquillity, that divine state of blessedness which man generally holds as the highest mode of being.

But if tranquillity brings happiness to men, then what, asks Pyrrho, leads men to tranquillity? How are men to achieve that imperturbable serenity so coveted by Democritus? This is a question Pyrrho has thought about long and hard, for the answer to it has great significance for man. It can set him on the right path toward his goal.

The Problem

Pyrrho has been forced to ask a simple and honest question: *Why have so few managed to achieve the goal?* One might think that people would be content, given that the majority of them seem to agree that tranquillity brings the happiness, or flourishing life, which is man's goal. But the problem is that most people are *not* happy. On the contrary, they are generally troubled and discontented.

How could this be so? Pyrrho explains it as follows. People, he says, want to obtain good and to avoid or escape evil. But success in such an undertaking implies *being able to determine* good and bad, to make correct judgements concerning them. However, this is impossible, Pyrrho insists. The experience of the dogmatic schools shows this. It is necessary only to witness their chaos of conflicting views, each school thinking itself right and all the others wrong! How is one to choose from such a tangle of opinions that which is closest to truth? Even if one could do so, the very process of attempting to determine the truth about good and bad things in our lives causes great anxiety.

One must ask, says Pyrrho, what is the cause of such widespread discontent? There is no more important question in the face of men's failure to live flourishing lives. And the answer is surprisingly simple. In believing things to be either good or bad, or true or false – that is to say, in the very act of making a judgement about such things – men are destined to suffer. Furthermore, they are bound to feel anguish from a lack of those allegedly good things or from the presence of things presumed to be bad. What, then, is the solution? At first glance, the problem may seem to be insoluble, given that the philosophers of the various schools have so far failed to bring about widespread happiness. Yet there is a way.

The Way
Pyrrho is presently meditating. It is an exercise of the spirit; its aim is to take him beyond a merely human viewpoint, to elevate him to a more encompassing perspective. He begins by repeating to himself a *mantram*, an inner discourse, which is an emblem of his philosophy: "This is no better than that." From time to time he alters its form, so that, while its essence remains the same, it becomes "Neither this nor that," or "One thing is not preferable to another," or "All things are of equal value." The mantrams and the arguments Pyrrho uses to justify his way of living are for him a gateway through which the normal human limits recede and a more expansive, divine perspective is approached.

It is the suspension of judgement concerning the truth or falsity of things that best characterizes both the thought and the action of Pyrrho and his followers. Thus Pyrrho does not yield to the desire to comprehend the truth about things, or to determine their goodness or badness. He holds himself in a state of *aphasia*, complete silence, and he diminishes anxiety by an act of *epoche*, suspension of judgement. And carried along with this suspension is the peace of mind which brings to him the happiness that is man's natural goal. But at the heart of all this lies a way of being that exembodies Pyrrho's fundamental attitude toward the world: he is utterly *adiaphoros*, indifferent. It is indifference which is the core of his practical wisdom, for it constitutes the only sure pathway to *ataraxia*: the blessed tranquillity of the gods.

Thus, says Pyrrho, let us *describe* things, but let us not attempt to *judge* them, since we can never know with certainty the truth or falsity of things. This need not concern us, though, for indifference and the tranquillity which follows it like a shadow free us from a need to inquire or discuss such things any further. If we believe things to be either good or bad, we may suffer from a lack of those good things or from the presence of bad things; or we may be anxious lest we lose good things and fall into bad. But indifference holds us back from passionate action; and the consequent quenching of desire leads to the tranquillity that brings happiness in the face of life's uncertainties.

What, then, must we do, asks Pyrrho. Live indifferently!

The Discourse

Those who know Pyrrho also know that he is perfectly capable of defending his philosophy and his way of living, which in truth are one. He has a discourse to justify his philosophy and to constantly renew his own choice of it as a way of being in the world. Many are the reasons he gives to convince himself and others of the truth of his mantram – "No more this than that" – which is but a verbal expression of the indifference he practises daily and which lies at the heart of his philosophy. As perception is both relative and subjective, says Pyrrho, it must be doubted.

But doubts are fortified by reasons, and Pyrrho offers reasons for adopting *epoche*, for suspending his judgement. And his followers are also fully capable of defending sceptical philosophy. Even now his disciple Timon of Phlius is eagerly crafting *silloi*, or satirical poems, designed to refute the Athenian dogmatists of the various schools.

Pyrrho notes that there is always a conflict of opinions among humans, and he cites the many schools of philosophy that have disagreed with one another, each thinking itself right and the others wrong. But Pyrrho says that we can never tell which, if any, of them is right, and he gives evidence against the senses and against reason to demonstrate this. He points to the following obstacles to accurate judgements concerning things.

✳

The senses provide us with illusory perceptions of things – who has never experienced such illusions? How then are we to know things truly?

Everything is mixed together by nature and each thing is related to all other things. How is it possible to know either the totality or any single part?

Different animals experience things differently. Who can say which perception of a given thing is to be preferred?

Similarly, our sensory perceptions differ in accordance with our own states of being or situation. When are we perceiving rightly?

And again, our perceptions vary according to our different points of view. Which point of view is correct?

Customs and religious practices vary greatly from place to place. How can one determine which set of practices is best?

✳

These are but a few of the many reasons Pyrrho cites to convince others that suspension of judgement is the appropriate response to the flawed reports of the senses.

As for reasoning, Pyrrho asserts that the syllogism of Aristotle is always a circular argument, for the conclusion is already present in the premisses. If "Socrates is a man" and if "all men are mortal," then we can conclude that "Socrates is mortal." Yet this conclusion does not constitute new knowledge, for it is already contained in the premisses. Hence the syllogistic form of argument can tell us nothing we don't already know about the truth or falsity of things.

Pyrrho goes further in criticizing reason. He says that *all* proof involves an infinite regress. A conclusion is derived from premisses which themselves are unproved, or hypothetical. In order to be certain we would have to prove each premiss. But this would mean deriving it from other appropriate premisses, which themselves would have to be proved. This process would go on *ad infinitum*. Hence, we cannot possibly establish certain knowledge through a proof based on human reason.

Pyrrho also insists that every argument concerning the truth of things can be opposed by an equally strong counterargument. Yet, in spite of all this, reason is not without some value, for it is critical reason which has guided Pyrrho to the indifference at the heart of his philosophy.

There are more arguments at Pyrrho's disposal, but equally there are other aspects to his philosophical discourse, particularly the constant self-dialogue – an exercise of the spirit, one which transforms him and renews at each moment his choice of the philosophical life.

The Life
These are uncertain times, times of upheaval. Witness how Alexander's Empire has given way to three new kingdoms. Who can say where things will go from here? Yet Pyrrho the *Skeptikos* remains serene, cleaving to that single word which adequately encompasses his attitude toward the world: *adiaphoros*, indifferent.

Some say that Pyrrho *never* distinguishes bad from good things, dangerous from safe situations, painful from pleasant sensations, inferior from superior acts – even death from life. But the truth of the matter is that Pyrrho retains enough common sense to take steps to protect himself from possible harm posed by carts or precipices or ferocious dogs, as well as to make everyday decisions in the common fashion. However, when it comes to the judgements of those such as the dogmatic philosophers, he is steadfastly indifferent. Yet he does not reject the world – he is happy in it (was not his own teacher Anaxarchus noted for his decidedly happy demeanour?). What Pyrrho rejects is *desire*. Thus he lives by appearances – that is, the customs and laws of his society – following his natural inclinations and abstaining from judgements concerning the truth or falsity of things. He applies his senses and his reason accordingly, eating when hungry and drinking when thirsty.

So Pyrrho continues to live simply, though not in the least through ignorance but rather through philosophy. His meditative discourse is a constant spiritual exercise, and he is often seen walking through the city reciting his mantrams aloud. At other times he seeks solitude and repeats them silently to himself. He possesses that *autarcheia*, or self-sufficiency, which was the emblem of Diogenes the Cynic, and he is utterly undisturbed by external circumstances. It is fitting, therefore, that Pyrrho has given to his fellow citizens that which more than anything else constitutes his philosophy – his *agoge*, or way of being in the world.

In such a manner philosophy teaches us to live by appearances and to reject dialectic concerning truth and falsity, good and evil, the ultimate nature of things, for such dialectic brings only disturbance to the soul. Pyrrho's philosophy, on the other hand, is a pathway to serenity and happiness. In the end, therefore, philosophy takes us to where we no longer need philosophical discourse – it is sufficient merely to *live* philosophically – that is, to live a life that embodies at every moment the supreme practical wisdom of indifference, whose shadow is that blessed tranquillity that mirrors the state of the gods. In such a manner, one secures the happiness of the *eudaimon*, or flourishing, life – a life like that of Pyrrho of Elis.

XIX
DEATH IS
NOTHING TO US

Empty is the argument of the philosopher through which no suffering is healed, for just as there is no benefit in medicine which does not heal the body, so there is no benefit in philosophy which does not heal the soul.

EPICURUS

Prelude

Epicurus was born of Athenian parents on the island of Samos in 341 BC. He taught philosophy at Mytilene and at Lampsacus, before purchasing a garden at Athens in 306 BC for 80 minae. There he founded a school and taught until his death in 270 BC. His school was open to women and slaves and became the most vilified school in the ancient world. The Christians, in particular, regarded the Epicureans as anathema because they denied the existence of a benevolent Creator, denied immortality, and affirmed the values of the material world. Objective knowledge of the material world was seen by the Epicureans as liberation from ignorance and superstition, and provided the possibility of living a flourishing life based on a correct view of reality.

The basic tenets of Epicureanism were threefold: empiricism, *the theory that sense-perception is the basis of our knowledge of reality;* hedonism, *the view that pleasure is the natural good for man; and* atomism, *the theory that all things are formed by the combining and separating of indivisible units, or atoms. Epicurus postulated random deviations from straight-line motion as a result of the atoms' inherent nature, thus providing an element of indeterminacy, or freedom, within the world. Since nothing comes out of nothing, atoms, the material foundation of all that exists, were seen as eternal and indestructible.*

The emblem of Epicureanism was an ethical one: the tetrapharmakos, *or fourfold remedy or therapy.* There is nothing to fear in gods; there is nothing to feel in death; good can be attained; evil can be endured. *For the Epicureans good was identified with pleasure, but not sensuous pleasure – rather, the serene contemplative pleasure of the gods:* ataraxia, *or tranquillity. Evil, on the other hand, was identified with pain of body or soul. Those who internalize the* tetrapharmakos *become like the gods in their blessedness, falling short of them only through their mortality. The ideal life is quiet, withdrawn, yet just, honourable, and pleasant, brimming over with friendship – Epicurus himself was a friend to countless others – and overseen by prudence, or practical wisdom.*

Although Epicurus is said to have written some three hundred books, only three letters and numerous sayings have been preserved. On his death in 270 BC, he was succeeded as leader of the school by Hermarchus, followed by Polystratus. Later disciples were Lucretius, Philodemus of Gadara, and Diogenes of Oenoanda. It is said that although many disciples in other schools left or changed their allegiance, few Epicureans did so. Epicureanism lasted as a significant influence on Graeco-Roman life from the fourth century BC until the fifth century AD; later it became a major influence on modern science and humanism, after its rediscovery in the sixteenth and seventeenth centuries.

DEATH IS NOTHING TO US

Athens, c. 270 BC

Characters

Epicurus (*a philosopher; founder of the Epicurean school of the Garden, at Athens*)
Colotes, Hermippus, Herodotus, Leonteus, Menoeceus, Parakaleos, Pythocles (*male Epicurean disciples*)
Leontion, Themista (*female Epicurean disciples*)
Mys (*a slave*)
Demetrius (*a servant*)

Scene

The Epicurean Garden at Athens. Demetrius is filling a bronze bathing tub. Epicurus' disciples and friends have gathered, as they regularly do, to discuss philosophy. Epicurus has already told them that this will be the last day of his life, and both they and the Master have expressed a wish to spend it together.

EPICURUS (*exuberantly*): Well, come now, my fellow-philosophers and good friends – you with whom I have shared the communal life of the Garden! Let us speak to each other about philosophy while Demetrius fills the tub with warm water. He too will join our discussion once the tub is filled, for he is as much a philosopher, a lover of wisdom, as any of us.

LEONTEUS (*uneasily*): Parakaleos was just saying how he feels honoured that you asked us to be with you today, on –

EPICURUS: – the last day of my life. Ah, yes.

LEONTEUS (*relieved*): Precisely. I'm sure we all feel the same, for you are our beloved Master and the kindest friend we shall ever have.

EPICURUS: Whom else should I wish to be with on such a day but those who have shared so much with me. As you all know, I have been beset with extreme agony at times during the past fourteen days – kidney stones are among the most painful of maladies, you may be assured – but I have set against such pain my memories of enjoyable conversations with you and others of my friends and pupils. Such thoughts have taken me away from agony into that domain of serene pleasure, where the true good for man resides.

HERODOTUS (*tentatively*): Master, how can we help on such a day as this?

EPICURUS (*reassuringly*): There is nothing to be afraid of or ashamed of, my young friend, for death is a natural separation of the atoms of which we are composed. You all know this as a fundamental principle of our philosophy, and therefore you know well the place of death within that philosophy which we share. In any case, I have lived a long life: it was seventy-one years ago that I was born, on the island of Samos, birthplace of

Pythagoras the sage.

HERODOTUS: But we have never lost such a friend as you. I think this is a feeling we all share, one that tests our philosophy to the limit. For it is a fine thing to repeatedly say that death is nothing to us, but when the one who has guided us to the highest philosophy is about to leave us forever –

EPICURUS (*gently*): I understand. Yet, however different from other men I may be, my state after death will not be so. Nor will yours be, when it comes. For you all know the meaning of our meditation: *Death is nothing to us*. And therefore you will understand my present wish when I say that today, on the last day of my life in this realm where humanity dwells, I want to discuss philosophy with my friends.

To be sure, in the first place I wish to know that I am leaving the Garden in good hands! But, more than this, I want to strengthen your resolve through philosophy, so that you will not feel more than a proper measure of pain at my departure from you, and that you will continue to spread the rational philosophy of pleasure and universal friendship after I am gone. Share each other's suffering always with a thoughtful concern rather than with lamentation. And rest assured that although I shall depart from this world, my atoms returning to that vast atomic sea that is the cosmos, I shall exist no more and hence shall sense nothing. But remember me, and the many times I have told you, "Sweet is the memory of a departed friend."

LEONTION: None sweeter than yours, Master.

EPICURUS: For that sentiment I thank you. (*To the others*) Leontion is living proof that women are quite as capable of philosophy as are men – no matter what Aristotle said. (*They all gesture in agreement.*)

But let me bid you remember why such a memory is so sweet.

LEONTION: Because it keeps alive within a woman the vision of a friend, and thereby strengthens her will to strive for that tranquillity which is the essence of our philosophy.

EPICURUS: As indeed I myself have been helped for a long time now by my own memories of philosophers who have gone before me and yet whom I still feel beside me as if they were alive.

And this I know to be true also of all of you, my friends, on whom I count for that feeling of security should I be in need. No matter that I am strong and seldom in need of help: it is nonetheless there, *whenever I should need it*. And that is the best of friendship's worth. For we all know that friendship begins in mutual need, but then, later, becomes something more, something good in itself.

You remember, no doubt, how often I have said, "Of all things which wisdom brings to a man to help make his life happy, greatest of value *by far*, is friendship." You also remember, I am sure, that I have never said merely "the greatest," but always "the greatest *by far*." That is how important friendship is; and that is why I have spoken of the "dance of friendship around the world," the only dance that brings the security from others which leads us to the highest tranquillity, *ataraxia*, the gateway to the *eudaimon*, or flourishing, life. For what other way is there to gain such security? If I make an enemy, I must constantly be on my guard; if I make a friend, I am given an extra hand in my time of trouble, and I give mine in return. Together we can share our troubles and our joys. We can share, in a word, the chance miracle of our earthly existence, the only existence there is for us. So, if you will, keep me alive in your memory and let me continue to do my work.

But now, let me hear from you. Tell me, or ask me, anything about our philosophy. Let us share what we have learned, our beliefs and our practices, in our last moments together. So, let me begin by asking you about our common philosophy. What is it? If someone were to ask you, what would you reply?

HERMIPPUS: Our philosophy is…well, I would start by saying, simply, a *therapeia*.

EPICURUS: And what do you mean by that?

THEMISTA: He means that philosophy is of no use if it does nothing to heal the soul, to console those in anguish – if it offers no help in living a good, which is to say happy, life.

EPICURUS: Well said. (*Turning to the others*) In Themista we have yet more evidence in our community that women are quite as good at mastering philosophical precepts as are their male counterparts. It is a pity that Aristotle never allowed women to study at the Lyceum.

But now, who will tell us of the nature of this therapy?

MYS: It consists of four strands in our philosophy, each one being in itself a *consolatio*, a healing balm.

EPICURUS: And now a slave, Mys, whose name means "Mouse," shows us that to true Philosophy it makes no difference from which class one comes, for She accepts one and all. Perhaps our openness is why we have become the most vilified of all the schools. But that may be a good sign, after all. (*He smiles.*) For if anything ought to be avoided, it is the culture of the multitude. It is far better that we live our lives away from the violence and chaos of civil society, from the vicissitudes of public life – that we live unseen, as it were.

But, pray tell us, "Mouse," what are the four strands, and how do they help us in our lives? And, while you are thinking about this, perhaps you can tell us something about the proper knowledge of reality. Is this not important as well? Or does it matter only that we feel happy?

MYS: It does matter that we feel happy, for that is the *telos*, the goal of human life. And we can achieve such a goal only through *hedone*, pleasure, but pleasure, mind you, of the highest sort, the kind the gods experience: we call it *ataraxia*, or tranquillity. But we also understand from our investigation of nature what the world is really like. It is at bottom naught but atoms in the void, as Democritus taught; but what he did not teach is that the combination and separation of atoms occur because of random variations in the motion of some atoms, due to an inherent cause. From this process are born all things: men, animals, plants, rocks, the earth itself, and the very cosmos. And from this process also comes the freedom of humanity, for not all things are fixed by nature; and with such freedom goes a responsibility for actions.

Thus, a correct understanding of the world is the essential foundation of our fourfold therapy, or philosophy; for ultimately our philosophy is nothing more than living a life in accord with a correct understanding of the world, based on our senses and our reason. That is precisely why we study nature, observe the heavens, think on the connections among things, for if we know what the world is, our reason will tell us how best to live in it. And our senses are never wrong: it is our judgement that sometimes fails. Hence, we must see to it that we acquire the means to make prudent judgements concerning things.

EPICURUS: You have expressed yourself well, my friend. You are a true philosopher and one, I might add, who fully deserves the freedom that my will bestows on you, as well as on Nicias, Lycon, and Phaedrium. But let us get back to the four strands of our philosophy. Do you wish to continue?

MYS: Perhaps I should ask Menoeceus to provide an answer to this question, for we all know of the excellent letter you wrote to him explaining the fourfold therapy, whose healing power concerns the gods, death, good, and evil. I have discussed this with Menoeceus, and he has improved my understanding.

EPICURUS: Very well. Menoeceus, can you tell us what we wish to know?

MENOECEUS: I shall do my best, Master. Let me say first that the fourfold therapy tells us that *there is nothing to fear in the gods*, and that *there is nothing to feel in death*. Furthermore, we may rest assured that *it is easy to attain good* and equally *easy to endure or avoid evil*. Each of the parts of the fourfold therapy functions as a *consolatio*, dissolving our fears, assuring us of happiness if only we tread the right path.

EPICURUS: Well said, Menoeceus. Now, we all have a common-sense idea of gods and death, but what are we to make of good and evil? What shall we take them to be? Parakaleos, as your name means "comfort" or "encourage," perhaps you can bring me some encouragement on my last day by assuring me that you will carry on with an understanding of our philosophy.

PARAKALEOS: Good is pleasure, Master; and evil is pain.

EPICURUS: How do you know this?

PARAKALEOS: Consider the infant placed in an uncomfortable position, or deprived of its mother's milk. What does it want? Only that the discomfort be removed – that is, by being placed in a comfortable position or by being given milk at its mother's breast. The discomfort is pain, or evil; its removal brings pleasure, or good.

EPICURUS (*noticeably pleased*): My friend, you are an excellent witness who has brought me comfort and encouragement – that is to say, pleasure. We shall hear more about good and evil soon enough. But now let us discuss the first strand or remedy, or, if you please, consolation. So let us ask, first of all, are the gods what men commonly take them to be?

THEMISTA: The gods of the many are gods we must deny, for the many are an impious lot, creating gods as vulgar as themselves.

COLOTES: Do you then deny utterly the existence of gods?

THEMISTA: That is a standard charge against the Epicurean philosophers of the Garden: *atheism*. It is well known that we deny the gods of the multitude, but we do not deny the existence of gods, for there are indeed gods. Nature has imprinted on our minds the conception of gods as existent, immortal, and blessed; and without such a notion we could not speak meaningfully about them. They are not, however, incorporeal, as the many insist, but are fashioned out of atoms, as are all things, though atoms of the finest, most subtle character.

Being blessed, as they are, they neither reward humans in this life nor punish them after death. In fact, it is their blessed character which serves as a model to us, showing us the way to tranquillity and the flourishing life that follows in its wake.

PYTHOCLES: But have not the gods created the cosmos and do they not keep it working?

THEMISTA: They have not created it, nor do they govern it. The universe has always existed, and it is self-regulating. To be involved in either creation or regulation of the cosmos would detract from the gods' absolute imperturbability, their utter serenity, in which case they would not be gods.

EPICURUS: Would that the gods could protect us from such impious views of them; but no, it is up to ourselves to regard them rightly. When we do so, we see there is nothing to fear in gods. We can allay our concerns and continue those practices which advance us toward the tranquil life.

DEMETRIUS: (*gently*) The tub is filled, Master.

EPICURUS: Good. Come join our discussion. Perhaps you can help us by – have you heard Themista's explanation?

DEMETRIUS: I have.

EPICURUS: Then tell us why we should have any interest in gods that have no interest in us, that can neither harm nor help us.

DEMETRIUS: Well, if I understand rightly, it is simply that the gods are for us an ideal to whose blessedness we may aspire, and, in doing so, guide our own actions thereby.

EPICURUS: Excellent. Then it is apparent that we do not have any cause whatever to fear gods. Though they cannot help us directly, they do so indirectly whenever we hold them in mind as blessed beings whose tranquillity we can imitate. In doing this, and in performing all the exercises which lead to divine serenity, we become, as it were, gods ourselves. For our lives become blessed like theirs, remaining inferior only in duration. This is why the gods take pleasure in looking upon us as we strive to be like them.

Thus, we can conclude that it is not we who are impious, but rather those who affirm of the gods what the multitude incorrectly believes about them. And *there is nothing to fear in gods* – this is the *consolatio*, or therapy – for they cannot harm us; but by correctly understanding their nature, we are able to aspire to that blessedness of which they are the supreme exemplars.

But what now of death, that most unjustly feared of all events. How are we to account for the fear? And how is it that we dare to say – as indeed we do in the second remedy of our fourfold therapy – that *death is nothing to us?* This is, I suppose, a question most relevant today, since for me it is the last of days. If you are wondering how I know this to be my last day, I can only say that my body has been constantly telling me so. I am in the same extreme pain I have suffered for the past fourteen days and I know that my time to depart is very near.

(*To Demetrius*) Well, let me not see your effort wasted: I shall get into the tub now, while the water is still warm. In a little while I shall ask for a large drink of unmixed wine. Meanwhile, let us get back to our second strand, or therapy. (*To all*) How is it possible for us to say what, at first glance, seems utterly contradictory: *Death is nothing to us?* (*Epicurus climbs into the tub.*)

COLOTES: It becomes possible only when we correctly understand death; and this becomes possible only when we use our senses and our reason wisely. When we do so, we realize that good and evil imply awareness. Hence, if death is taken to be bad for us, we must in some sense be aware of it. However, when death is come, we are *not*; and when we *are*, death is not yet come. In other words, death is the privation of all awareness, the utter end of our existence as sentient beings, though, of course, the atoms of which we are made continue their eternal dance.

Now, in all of this there is nothing to fear, for pain and anguish are part of life, not of death. It is rather the *expectation* that causes distress: death itself can cause nothing, for after death there is no longer any subject who can experience anything. We can even say that a proper understanding that death is nothing to us actually makes the mortality of life more enjoyable, not by adding an unlimited time to life but by removing the yearning for immortality.

EPICURUS: But what of a life that is short? Is this not something suitable for lamentation, as the multitude says?

COLOTES: Not at all, for it is the most pleasant rather than the longest life that we should prefer. The wise will choose first and foremost to make their lives pleasant.

EPICURUS: And how should the young and the old differ in their attitude toward death?

COLOTES: Those who admonish the young to live well, and the old to make a good end, speak foolishly, not merely because life is desirable, but because the same exercise at once teaches a man to live well and to die well. We must remember that life resides in the present moment; the future is neither wholly ours nor wholly not ours, so that neither must we count upon it as quite certain to come nor despair of it as quite certain not to come.

EPICURUS: Colotes has shown by his explanation to us that he understands perfectly the second *consolatio*, or therapy of anguish, which our philosophy bestows on the disciple. If we are to make these consolations part of ourselves, however, we shall have to perform those exercises of the spirit which lead to that end. But let us continue with the next two remedies. Then we shall round out our discussion by considering the exercises themselves.

HERMIPPUS: To speak of the last two remedies – that *good is easy to attain* and that *evil is easy to endure* – we must surely speak first of desires. For every time we satisfy a desire we bring ourselves pleasure or pain – that is to say, good or evil. Therefore, if we understand the nature of desires, we are better able to act so as to maximize pleasure and minimize pain in our lives.

EPICURUS: A good start, Hermippus. Can you take us further along this line of thinking? Are there different kinds of desires and, if so, how can we act wisely with regard to them?

HERMIPPUS: I shall try my best. First, let us reflect that of desires some are natural, others groundless; and that of the natural desires some are necessary, some only natural. Of the necessary desires, some are necessary for happiness, some for ridding the body of discomfort, some merely to prolong life. A natural and necessary desire, for example, is for food and drink. A natural but not necessary desire is for an extravagant table. A groundless desire is for riches. One who understands all of this will direct every choice and aversion toward health of the body and tranquillity of mind, the latter of which is, as we have already heard today, the pathway to man's ultimate goal: *eudaimonia*, or happiness.

EPICURUS: You have explained this well, my friend, but you have not yet made a connection between desires and aversions, on the one hand, and pleasure and pain, on the other.

HERMIPPUS: You are quite right, Master, but now I shall attempt to do so. Consider how pleasure is our first and kindred good, that which alone can lead us to a blessed life. And as the end of all our actions is to be free from pain and fear, once we have attained such a state we are tranquil, no longer in need of anything else. We have, in other words, achieved our true end.

EPICURUS: Clearly you have in mind an unusual idea of pleasure, if it is merely the removal of pain and fear.

HERMIPPUS: It is contrary to the usual notion, to be sure. Our pleasure is not that of the prodigal; nor is it the pleasure of sensuality. Of course, we Epicureans are often accused of such pleasure-seeking by others, through ignorance or prejudice, or wilful misrepresentation. But by pleasure we simply mean the absence of pain in the body and of trouble in the soul. This is no strange conception of pleasure: it is the very pleasure of the gods themselves. For it is not an unbroken succession of drinking-bouts and of merrymaking, not sexual love, not the enjoyment of fish and other delicacies of a luxurious table, which produces a pleasant life: it is sober reasoning, searching out the grounds of every choice and avoidance, and banishing those beliefs through which the greatest disturbances take possession of the soul.

Thus, even though pleasure is our natural good, we do not choose every pleasure; nor do we avoid every pain. Sometimes we pass over pleasures, knowing that a greater pain follows in their wake. And at times pain is superior to pleasure, if submission to pain brings greater pleasure as a consequence. Therefore, of all this the greatest good is that which helps us to properly exercise choice and avoidance: I speak of *prudence*, or practical wisdom. That is why prudence is more precious than all the other virtues; for one cannot lead a life of pleasure which is not at the same time a life of prudence, honour, and justice; nor can one lead a life of prudence, honour, and justice which is not at the same time a life of pleasure. In short, the virtues are inseparable from a pleasant life.

PYTHOCLES: I understand what you say, but let me ask you where the last two remedies are in all of this?

HERMIPPUS: I shall tell you. Good — that is, pleasure — is easy to attain. Knowing that pleasure is simply the absence of pain in the body and of trouble in the soul, we can see that a simple diet and, in general, a simple life will produce it. We extol the virtue of *autarcheia*, self-sufficiency, which Diogenes prized above all else, because it allows us to be contented with little; and if, on occasion, we are able to feast, so be it, as long as we do not live in expectation of such extravagance, which can only make us dependent on things outside ourselves. Furthermore, it seems evident that those who stand least in need of luxuries are best able to appreciate them when they become available.

Add to this the boon of friendship, a community of shared joys and of mutual aid, and you will be able to see why we have here another remedy: *good is easy to attain*. It also follows from all of this that evil is easy to avoid or to endure, for when good is present, evil is absent. Even in those cases where illness strikes the body —

EPICURUS: — as indeed it has done in my case.

HERMIPPUS: Yes, even then it is possible to withstand evil, just as our Master has done. For generally if pain is extreme, it is short-lived; if it lasts for a long time, its intensity is slight. So we can state with some confidence our fourth remedy: that *evil can be endured*.

EPICURUS: Well done, Hermippus. Now, I shall not burden you with a description of my agonies over the past fourteen days, except to repeat that the pleasure of my discussions with all of you and others during that time has greatly outweighed any evil I have suffered. I have still managed to maintain my state of *ataraxia*, blessed tranquillity, during this time — even now, as I ready myself to depart, still in pain.

But let me congratulate all of you on having spoken so eloquently about our common philosophy. I shall leave you shortly, and with the knowledge that the Garden community will flourish as will your own lives.

(Epicurus motions to Demetrius to bring him unmixed wine. The rest, including Epicurus' brothers and the other few who have been content to listen

thoughtfully to the discussion without taking part, gather close to the Master, touching his arms and shoulders, stroking his head.)

Before I go, let me summarize for you the fourfold remedy, or therapy of anguish, which we have discussed on the last day of my life. (*He looks at Leontion, thinking of her steadfast devotion to philosophy, recalling to mind the excellent treatise she wrote against Theophrastus.*) Let me describe the woman who holds it in her heart. Her beliefs about the gods are truly pious; she is ever fearless of death; she understands the end fixed for humanity by nature and knows how easily the limit of good things can be attained; she knows also how evil can be avoided or, if necessary, endured. She knows that some things happen of necessity, others by chance, still others through our own agency. It is the latter which, through the piety of such a one, are guided by practical wisdom and encompass both her freedom and her responsibility. None can surpass her.

(Demetrius hands him the wine; Epicurus takes a draught.)

Finally, let me exhort you to continue to practise the exercises I have taught you. By this I mean such things as memorizing the precepts of our philosophy; studying the form and the inner workings of nature; meditating on the true and blessed character of the gods; thinking on death as the utter end of a human life, thereby making all the more precious the present instant; holding constantly in mind a vision of the sage, wise in all things; and learning to turn the mind from painful thoughts to pleasant remembrances. Practise these alone or together with friends; and most of all, let friendship dance among yourselves and out into the world, easing your anguish and spreading your joy.

Remember that our task is to live life well, and it is philosophy's role to help us to do so. Therefore no age is too old or too young for philosophy, since no age is too old or too young for health of the soul, as Socrates used to say. To say that the time for studying philosophy has not yet come, or has come and gone, is rather like saying that the time for happiness is not yet here, or has already gone. (*Epicurus, wincing in pain, tosses back the rest of the wine.*)

I have just this morning written a letter to Idomeneus, who has been so good to me and to philosophy, asking him to look after Metrodorus' children. To the rest of you, my friends and fellow-philosophers, and to those who are not here with us today, I bid you goodbye. The gods be with you; be like the gods.

XX
PHILOSOPHER-SLAVE, PHILOSOPHER-KING

Nothing is inferior to love of pleasure, and love of gain and pride.
Nothing is superior to magnanimity, and gentleness, and love of
mankind, and beneficence.

EPICTETUS

Love all that comes to you spun out of the threads of your destiny. For
what could be more suitable?

MARCUS AURELIUS

Prelude

*Stoicism, which began alongside Scepticism and Epicureanism after the death
of Alexander the Great in 323 BC, became the most influential philosophy in the
Roman Empire prior to the rise of Christianity. Its name derives from the Stoa
Poikile, or "Painted Colonnade," at Athens. There the early Stoics carried on
their discourse, led first by Zeno (c. 336-264 BC) of Citium, Cleanthes (c. 331-
232 BC) and Chrysippus (c. 280-205 BC); then followed by Panaetius (c. 180-
110 BC) and Posidonius (c. 135-50 BC).*

*Along with Seneca (c. 5 BC-AD 65), the chief representatives of Roman
Stoicism were the slave Epictetus (c. AD 55-135) and the emperor Marcus
Aurelius (AD 121-180). Born at Hierapolis, Epictetus attended lectures of the
Roman Stoic Musonius Rufus. He later gained his freedom from his master, a
servant of Nero, and established a school at Nicopolis in southern Epirus after
Emperor Domitian closed the philosophical schools in Rome in AD 89. Although
Epictetus wrote nothing, his disciple Arrian preserved his lectures, of which we*

possess four surviving books of the Discourses *as well as the* Enchiridion, or Manual.

Marcus Aurelius *became emperor in* AD *161. As a youth he studied Epictetus' works and followed his ethical philosophy. He learned to distinguish those things within one's power from those not within one's power, to act or refrain with respect to the former and to accept with equanimity the latter. His life and his philosophy were one and the same, and thus he sought to rule like a true philosopher-king. This last of the great Stoics died in camp on the Danubian frontier of the Empire.*

The Stoics were materialists and pantheists: they saw the world as entirely corporeal, and permeated and governed by an immanent Logos *or universal* Reason *consisting of the most subtle matter. Following Heraclitus, they posited fire as the basic element of the world, ultimately responsible for the conflagrations which dissolve and re-create the cosmos at the end of each vast cosmological cycle or "world year." From Socrates they adopted the ethical principle that no harm can come to a good human being. The deeply spiritual tone of the Roman Stoics profoundly affected many early Christian thinkers, including Saint Augustine.*

PHILOSOPHER-SLAVE, PHILOSOPHER-KING

Evening, on the banks of the River Danube, c. AD *175*

In his tent, deep in meditation, Marcus Aurelius Antoninus, the emperor, has forgotten for the moment why he has come to this alien landscape, so remote from the heart of his philosophy. It has been several years now that Rome has been fighting the Quadi and Marcomanni, as well as other tribes, on the fringes of the Empire. Marcus has never had a great love for combat and bloodshed – witness his recent taming of the gladiatorial contests, in which the weapons used are now so blunt as to preclude the likelihood of serious injury or death – but he considers this battle an essential duty on behalf of the Empire, and it is a task he takes seriously.

Of course, there have been conflicts *within* the Empire as well. Recently, in northern Italy and southern Gaul, a deserter named

Maternus organized slaves and peasants into a force that struck terror into the hearts of the landowners of those regions. At about the same time, Avidius Cassius, governor of Syria, proclaimed himself emperor, but was slain by soldiers loyal to Marcus. When they brought to Marcus the head of the traitor, the emperor, disgusted, sent them straight away and ordered that the rebels be treated with clemency. His thoughts of these events bring to his mind a passage from Epictetus, the lame philosopher-slave.

> *Pittacus after being wronged by a certain person and having the power of punishing him let him go, saying, "Forgiveness is better than revenge: for forgiveness is the sign of a gentle nature, but revenge the sign of a savage nature."*

Perhaps it was this thought from the slave that inspired the emperor to forgive the Syrian trespassers, or perhaps it was Philosophy herself, through the manner in which She came to the emperor and transformed him into one who knows himself and who practises daily the spiritual exercise of governing with wisdom.

A youthful servant brings a taper and lights it for him. The ruler of the greatest of empires opens his journal and prepares to write down his thoughts. Flipping through the pages, he stops now and then to read an entry made at an earlier time: last month, last year, two years ago. This re-reading of old entries is an exercise of the spirit, a therapy of the soul, one he often practises. For Marcus, the journal itself is such an exercise.

He regards a previous entry and begins to read it as a meditation:

> *Of human life the time is but a point, and the substance a flux, and the perception dull, and the composition of the whole body subject to decay, and the soul a whirl, and fortune hard to divine, and fame a thing most dubious. And, to say all in a word, everything which belongs to the body is a stream, and what belongs to the soul is a dream and vapour, and life is a warfare and a stranger's sojourn, and after-fame is oblivion.*

It has been months, perhaps years, now since Marcus wrote these words, but they are ever fresh in his mind. They are, in fact, an essential part of a credo, of what he believes and lives each day – better still, each moment. He is all too aware of the precariousness of life, its brevity, man's ultimate fate: death of the body, and, for the soul, re-absorption into the universal Substance, either immediately or at the end of the cosmic cycle that brought this world into being.

He turns back to the first few entries of the journal. Noticing the familiar name of Rusticus, his law-tutor and friend, he begins to read.

> *From Rusticus I received the impression that my character required improvement and discipline; and from him I learned not to be led astray to sophistic emulation, nor to writing on speculative matters, nor to delivering little exhortations, nor to showing myself off as a man who practises much discipline, or does benevolent acts in order to make a display. I also learned to abstain from rhetoric, and poetry, and fine writing; and not to walk about in the house in my outdoor dress, nor to do other things of the kind; and to write my letters with simplicity, like the letter which Rusticus wrote from Sinuessa to my mother; and with respect to those who have offended me by words, or done me wrong, to be easily disposed to be pacified and reconciled, as soon as they have shown a readiness to be reconciled. And I learned to read carefully, and not to be satisfied with a superficial understanding of a book; nor hastily to give my assent to those who talk overmuch. And most of all I am indebted to him for being acquainted with the discourses of Epictetus, which he communicated to me out of his own collection.*

The last sentence strikes a chord in Marcus, and his thoughts turn again to Epictetus, the philosopher-slave, from whose works he has learned more than from anyone else. He does not find it strange that a slave – albeit a freed one – should be giving philosophy lessons to an emperor, which is to say, lessons in how to live one's life properly. Rather, he feels, in spite of his Stoicism, a pang of regret that the lame philosopher is no longer alive; for even though death is nothing to fear (this is one of many lessons he has learned from Epictetus), it would still be counted a great joy for the emperor to be able to discuss philosophy with his low-born Master. But Fate has not decreed such an encounter of like minds; Marcus is therefore thankful for Arrian's work in preserving his Master's lectures on philosophy. Through them the slave has taught the emperor the proper goal of the philosopher. Marcus recalls another passage from Epictetus.

> What do I care whether all things are composed of atoms, or of similar parts of fire and earth? For is it not enough to know the nature of good and evil, and the measures of desires and aversions, and also the movements toward things and from them; and to use these as rules to administer the affairs of life, but not to trouble ourselves about the things above us? For these things are perhaps incomprehensible to the human mind; and if any man should even suppose them to be in the highest degree comprehensible, what then is the profit of them, if they are comprehended? Must we not say that those men have needless trouble who assign these things as necessary to the philosopher's discourse? Is then also the precept written at Delphi superfluous, which is Know thyself? It is not so. And what is its meaning? It means direct attention to oneself.

In such a manner Marcus first learned the importance of the Delphic precept, and he has made it inseparable from his life. This is an emperor who knows himself, and who has directed sufficient attention to himself in order to transform himself into what his teacher and his own reason tell him he must become. His journal entry on the value of philosophy is but an extension of that of his Master, the slave. Searching for it, he finds it and begins to read.

> What then is that which is able to conduct a man? One thing and only one: Philosophy. But this consists in keeping the divine spirit within a man free from violence and unharmed, superior to pains and pleasures, doing nothing without purpose, nor yet falsely and

with hypocrisy, not feeling the need of another man's doing or not doing anything; and besides, accepting all that happens, and all that is allotted, as coming from that same Source as himself.

This, Epictetus' most important lesson, concerns the true nature of good and evil, and the role of philosophy in the life of man. He has taught Marcus the fundamental principle of ethics: that *moral virtue is what is good, and moral vice is what is evil.* The good man will be the philosopher who is able to think clearly, using the reason he possesses (which is but a spark of that universal Reason permeating all things), and who is thereby able to distinguish things within his power from those not within his power. The former alone – those things within our power – can be good or evil, and a man must act with understanding and good will concerning them: that is, *virtuously.* The latter – those things not in our power – cannot be good or evil, nor can they touch us but through our false opinion of them. When they are serenely accepted as belonging to the way of Nature, they are understood as part of the rational order of Providence and they lose all power to harm us in any way.

Of things some are in our power, and others are not. In our power are opinion, movement toward a thing, desire, aversion and, in a word, whatever are our own acts; not in our power are the body, property, reputation, offices and, in a word, whatever are not our own acts. And the things in our power are by nature free, not subject to restraint nor hindrance: but the things not in our power are weak, slavish, subject to restraint, in the power of others. Failure to understand all this and to act rightly will bring us only hindrance, lamentation, disturbance, and a propensity to blame both gods and men. Knowing all this allows us to act rightly and thereby to bring to ourselves freedom, happiness, tranquillity, and constancy; to live in accord with justice and law, to achieve temperance and every virtue.

Therefore seek not that the things which happen should happen as you wish; but wish the things which happen to be as they are, and you will have a tranquil flow of life.

This passage from Epictetus always puts Marcus in mind of his own brief entry on the subject. He does not need to turn to it in his journal, for he has long possessed it in memory – it has become a meditation that he frequently repeats to himself:

> *Take away your opinion, and then there is taken away the complaint, "I have been harmed." Take away the complaint, "I have been harmed," and the harm is taken away.*

Thus, from Epictetus Marcus has learned to recognize the true nature of things perceived, and to turn aside those which are false or unclear. Furthermore, he has learned to distinguish between those things which depend on us and those which do not; the former are those we can turn to virtuous purpose, the latter those we can but serenely accept. So it is that Marcus has long practised the exercise of limiting his desires and aversions, restricting them to those things which depend on him. He stands firm, ready always to accept everything that comes to him, knowing that it is part of a universal Reason which can bring him no harm if he but think of things truthfully. Continuing to peruse his journal, he comes across an entry which expresses most aptly his immediate resolve.

> *Be like the promontory against which the waves continually break, but it stands firm and tames the fury of the water around it. Unhappy am I because this has happened to me? Not so, but happy am I, though this has happened to me, because I continue free from pain, neither crushed by the present nor fearing the future. For such a thing as this might have happened to every man; but every man would not have continued free from pain on such an occasion. Will this which has happened prevent you from being just, magnanimous, temperate, prudent, secure against inconsiderate opinions and falsehood? Will it prevent you from having modesty, freedom, and everything else by the presence of which man's nature is fulfilled? Rather than "This is a misfortune," say "To bear this nobly is good fortune."*

In such a manner does Marcus Aurelius, Emperor of Rome, disciple of the slave Epictetus, practise the exercises that foster *objective judgement, virtuous action,* and *serene acceptance,* the threefold heart of his philosophy. He is reminded for a moment of Epicurus, who, when he was sick, never complained of his illness, but rather went on discussing philosophy with his visitors, his mind remaining clear and at ease even though fully aware of the ailment of his body. Marcus exhorts himself to be like the Master of the Garden in this respect. Turning the pages of his journal, the philosopher-king reviews the many threads he has woven into virtue's tapestry.

On man's *telos,* or goal:

> *Everything exists for some end, a horse, a vine. Why do you wonder? Even the sun will say, I am for some purpose, and the rest of the gods will say the same. For what purpose then are you? To enjoy pleasure? Will common sense allow this?*

On star-gods:

> *A man asks, "Where have you seen the gods?" and "How are you so sure of their existence that you feel able to worship them?" My answer is this: "They are perfectly visible in the night sky for anyone to see."*

On the good god within:

> *Remember that no matter what you do God is watching. In this way you will have a Power inside you ensuring that you never do wrong.*

On contentment:

> *He lives with the gods who constantly shows them a satisfied soul, one that lives in accord with that ruling spark of Reason which is given by Zeus to every man.*

On resolution toward virtue:

*Begin the morning by saying to yourself: Today I shall meet
with the busy-body, the ungrateful, arrogant, deceitful, envious,
unsocial. All these things happen to them by reason of their
ignorance of what is good and evil. But I who have seen the nature
of the good that it is beautiful, and of the bad that it is ugly, and
the nature of him who does wrong, that it is akin to me in that
it participates in the same Reason and the same portion of the
divinity, I can neither be injured by any of them – for no one can
fix on me what is ugly – nor can I be angry with my kinsman, nor
hate him. For we are made for co-operation, like feet, like hands, like
eyelids, like the rows of the upper and lower teeth. To act against
one another then is contrary to the law of Nature.*

On the creative Force:

*No longer only let your breathing act in concert with the air which
surrounds you, but let your intelligence also now be in harmony
with the Intelligence which embraces all things. For the Intelligent
Power is no less available to him who is willing to draw it to
himself than is the air for him who is able to breathe it.*

On the limit of discourse:

*No longer talk at all about what a good man ought to be; be such
a man.*

On the cosmopolitan life:

*Short is the little which remains to you of life. Live as on a
mountain. For it makes no difference whether a man lives there or
here, if he lives in the cosmopolis, the world-city. Let men see, let
them know a real man who lives according to Nature.*

On the dialectics of Nature:

Frequently consider the connexion of all things in the universe

*and their relation to one another. For in a manner all things are
implicated with one another, and all in this way are in sympathy
with one another.*

On Reason as master:

*Whatever this is that I am, it is a little flesh and breath, and the
ruling part. What is the flesh but blood and bones and a network
of nerves, veins, and arteries. And the breath also, air, not always
the same, but every moment renewed. But the third, the ruling part
— Reason — is what you must concentrate on.*

On conforming to Nature:

*This you must always bear in mind: the nature of the Whole,
your own nature, and how one is related to the other. Then hold in
mind that there is no one who hinders you from always doing and
saying the things which are according to the Nature of which you
are a part.*

As for death, that most feared event, Marcus understands that even
death is not to be dreaded, for it also is not in our power. It can
harm us only when our passions are not held in check by reason,
when we let ourselves believe that death is in some degree in our
power; and the philosopher-slave has taught the philosopher-king
that death has its own exercises which help to make it clear that
it is no concern of ours. If a good friend dies, one must think and
believe, "My friend has been returned to the universal Substance
out of which he came," and then one will not suffer pain. This is
an exercise which can be practised daily, but at first with inanimate
things we hold dear: if a favourite pot or vase accidentally breaks,
one must say to oneself, "It has been returned," and one will not
suffer.
  And Epictetus has also taught Marcus the constant exercise of
meditation on death:

Let death and exile and every other thing which appears dreadful
be daily before your eyes; but most of all death: and you will never
think of anything mean nor will you desire anything extravagant.

Thus has Marcus come to see death as part of Nature's infinite wisdom.

Death is such as generation is, a mystery of nature; a composition
out of the same elements, and a decomposition into the same; and
altogether not a thing of which any man should be ashamed, for
it is not contrary to the nature of a reasonable animal, and not
contrary to the reason of our constitution. You have existed as a
part of the Whole. You will disappear into that which gave you
birth, or rather you will be transmuted back into the universal
Reason.

The day has been long, and Marcus is tired. He returns to the empty page and prepares to enter tonight's meditation into his journal. He exhorts himself to seek repose in the present moment, that moment in which everything resides, and to be content with all that has, and will, come to him; to be honest and fair to all; to respect the divinity within. Thinking again of the philosopher-slave and the lessons he has learnt from him, he begins to write:

All those things at which you wish to arrive by a circuitous road,
you can have now, if you do not refuse them. And this means you
must take no notice of all the past, trust the future to Providence,
and direct the present with piety and justice: piety by acceptance
of your lot in life, for Nature designed it for you and you for it;
justice by honesty and forthrightness, and in action through respect
for the law and for the worth of each man.

Marcus closes his book just before the taper burns itself out, the substance of its little life transposed back into the universal Reservoir. He closes his eyes and begins to empty his mind, retreating to that inner sanctuary which every man possesses, would he but use it. The emperor ends the day by performing the spiritual exercise which serves to remind him of who he would become.

> *In the writings of the Ephesian philosophers there was this precept, constantly to think of someone of former times who practised virtue.*

As thoughts of the great Empire recede from his consciousness, Marcus Aurelius Antoninus, ruler of fifty million subjects, holds in his mind's eye a vision of Epictetus, the lame philosopher-slave, his true Master.

XXI
THE ONE

By the power of the Soul the manifold and diverse heavenly system is a unit; through soul this universe is a god; and the sun is a god because it is ensouled; so too the stars; and whatsoever we ourselves may be, it is all in virtue of soul.

PLOTINUS

Prelude

The Neoplatonist Plotinus, the last great Graeco-Roman philosopher, was born at Lycopolis, Egypt in AD 204 and died in Campania, in southern Italy, in AD 270. As a youth, he was educated in the Greek tradition, later studying philosophy for eleven years at Alexandria with Ammonius Saccas. He left Alexandria to join Emperor Gordian III on an expedition to the East, where he hoped to discover the wisdom of the Persian sages, but when Gordian was assassinated by his own soldiers, the expedition was abandoned and Plotinus fled to Antioch.

In AD 245 Plotinus settled in Rome and opened a school, attracting many students from a wide variety of professions. There he conducted classes and later began to write. After the age of fifty he began writing a series of short treatises. Upon his death these were arranged by his disciple Porphyry into six groups of nine essays, entitled The Enneads *(from the Greek "nine"), which together constitute both a handbook of salvation and an explanation of the spatio-temporal world in terms of the ineffable One, the eternal source of all being. As an aid to this account Plotinus uses the metaphor of "emanation" – in a logical, rather than temporal, sense. Much as the sun emanates light, the One emanates*

Nous, *which may also be called Mind, Spirit, Universal Reason, or Intellect. Through this latter emanates the World-Soul and all individual souls. The final emanation is matter, the lowest realm and the closest approach to non-being.*

Among Plotinus' sources are Pythagoras, Plato, Aristotle, and the Stoics; but Plato is clearly the main influence on his thinking. Plotinus rejuvenates Platonic metaphysics, deepens the mystical elements of Plato's anti-materialist philosophy, and creates one of the most complex and difficult, though fascinating, metaphysical systems ever invented. The purpose of mankind, according to Plotinus, is to ascend to the One through an ecstatic mystical experience in which the soul loses itself and merges with the divine. Although the mystical experience transcends rationality, and is in essence incomprehensible, Plotinus uses reason to argue that it is nonetheless the proper goal of man.

During Plotinus' lifetime the Roman Empire was beginning to break apart. His philosophy reflects a spiritual void within his world and, at the same time, expresses aspirations concerning an eternal world of Truth, Beauty, and Goodness. After his death, Plotinus exerted a considerable influence on Christian thinkers, including Saint Augustine. His last moments were spent in Campania patiently waiting for a visit from his friend the doctor Eustochius, who, when he finally arrived, was greeted with Plotinus' words: "I am striving to give back the Divine in myself to the Divine in the All." Apparently, as he spoke a snake crawled under his bed and crept into a hole in the wall. At that precise moment, Plotinus died.

THE ONE

Rome, c. AD 265

It has been for some time now clear to the philosopher Plotinus that the Empire is in decline. In recent years its frontiers have been assaulted by Franks, Moors, Sarmatians, and Goths, among other tribes, some of whom have formed confederacies so as to devastate and pillage the provinces more effectively. And the recent rise of Palmyra to prominence in the East has even further threatened the integrity of the Empire. Fourteen years have passed since the emperor Decius was killed in a Danubian encounter with the Goths; and Romans have not yet forgotten – however much they might wish to – the recent humiliating imprisonment of Emperor Valerian by the Persian King Shapur. In the brief span since Decius' death there have been four successive emperors, yet another indicator of the instability of the Empire.

Currently Rome is ruled by Valerian's son, Gallienus, who succeeded to power jointly with his father twelve years ago and who has ruled alone for the past five years. He is a soldier-emperor of considerable erudition who has instituted many reforms of benefit to the cities and, in addition to halting persecution of the Christians, has become a patron of culture as well as personal friend to Plotinus. Gallienus has also reformed relations between the Senate and the army, and has wisely placed the cavalry under the command of a single general. A wave of resentment is surging among the nobility, however, and soldiers loyal to the emperor have already been forced to suppress more than a few mutinies in a number of provinces. And there is yet another factor of concern: the continuing decline of urban populations as a result of the double scourge of pestilence and taxation.

In spite of all this, Plotinus calmly continues to extol the noblest values of Graeco-Roman culture. People, he says, must attend to their highest function and not allow evil to overcome them if they are to be happy in this life and, more than this, to ascend to union with the One at the heart of the world. They must choose between being oriented toward the lower realm of the body and the higher realm of the intellect. Like Pythagoras and Plato before him, Plotinus knows that the flourishing life lies at the end of an inward road of purification of the soul. Thus, one's life must come to embody one's philosophical discourse. If one speaks of the necessity of striving toward God, then one must restrain bodily desires, live a contemplative life, and act morally; withdraw inward and eliminate all excess, straighten what is crooked, cast light on darkness, and fashion within oneself a glow of beauty and a splendour of virtue. Only through such exercises can one hope to prepare for a mystical union with the divine. As Plotinus puts it, "'God' on the lips, without a good conduct of life, is but a word."

And so Plotinus has laboured to make his whole life one with his philosophy. Although he shuns pubic life, he is highly regarded by all who have met him; he makes friends easily, enemies not at all. His kindness is already legendary: he has taken into his household orphaned children of men and women of considerable social position, with all their property, and he has ensured the proper administration of everything. "Until the young people are able to take to philosophy," he says, "their property must be kept intact for them." And Plotinus has never failed to live up to this credo, for he labours strenuously to rise above the strife of fleshly existence. Furthermore, he is renowned both for his gentleness in all dealings and for his openness and availability to all who are in the least acquainted with him. In speaking, he is humble, devoid of pretension, and his lectures give the impression rather of easy conversation, the profound logic underlying them never intruding as a barrier to the listener. His writing is concise, yet inspired, and pregnant with ideas, its complexity tempered by its beauty; his disciples are convinced that his words have been overseen and guided by a divine hand.

Since founding his school at Rome twenty years ago, Plotinus has attracted many students from a wide variety of professions, including senators and members of the imperial household. In fact, not so long ago the Emperor Gallienus and his wife, Salonina, became favourably disposed to his plan to create in Campania a city called "Platonopolis," a model state based on Platonic principles, but opposition at court based on envy or spite ended the plan before it could begin. Nonetheless, Plotinus' following is a large one, and it includes many notable disciples: Amelius of Tuscany; Paulinus, a doctor of Scythopolis; Eustochius of Alexandria – also a doctor; Zoticus, a critic and poet; Zethos, an Arabian doctor at whose country house near Minturnae Plotinus often stays; and Castricius Firmus. Add to these several senators, among whom are Rogatianus, whose philosophical development prompted him to renouce his office and property, dismiss his slaves, abandon his house, and live instead with friends, taking but one meal every second day – a regime that has cured his gout and restored his health. And there is also Porphyry of Tyre, a close friend and keen disciple who came to him but two years ago, and who takes great interest in Plotinus' writings, as well as his lectures. He often speaks of the Master's gentle, though utterly convincing, manner of having converted him to true philosophy. It is Porphyry who has become entrusted with the task of organizing Plotinus' writings (his works are passed only to those within the close circle of his most trusted friends). In addition to these, there are also several women who have become greatly attached to Plotinus and to his philosophy, including Gemina and her daughter of the same name, and Amphiclea, wife of Ariston.

Plotinus is presently in his study sitting at his writing desk. He is remembering how, at the age of twenty-seven, he first felt a great passion for philosophy. It was then that he sought out the philosophers of Alexandria, but was disappointed with all of them until he heard Ammonius Saccas speak, after which he exclaimed, "This is the man I was looking for!" He stayed with Ammonius for eleven years before deciding to accompany the emperor Gordian III on his expedition to the East. There Plotinus had hoped to learn something of Persian and Indian philosophy, for he had heard of the Magi, the renowned Persian sages. He recalls how the expedition was cut short by the assassination of Gordian at the hands of his own soldiers, and how he was fortunate to escape to Antioch with his life. Shortly thereafter, at the age of forty, he came to Rome and founded his school. Here he began teaching and, later, putting his words down in order that others might learn the true nature of the Real.

The Reality of which Plotinus speaks and writes is completely contrary to that of Epicurus, for whom atoms and the void were the *arche*, or principle, of the world; for Plotinus, on the other hand, Reality consists of a hierarchy of three *hypostases* or basic substances. First, there is the One, limitless, undifferentiated, utterly tranquil – the eternal source of all things; the One is ineffable – words cannot describe it, but rather can only point to it. Below the One is *Nous*, or Intellect, an emanation from the One, directing itself toward It and, through contemplation, filled with It. Next comes Soul, an emanation from the One through Intellect, capable of turning toward and seeking the One. Matter itself is merely the lowest realm – a formless possibility taking form only under the direction of Soul, which in turn is dependent on Intellect, emanating from the One. Plotinus' rational discourse constitutes an eloquent extended argument for his metaphysical vision, and yet he offers more than mere theorizing, for he himself has risen on several occasions to unity with the One, the Fount of all that exists.

> *Many times it has happened: lifted out of the body into myself; becoming external to all other things and self-encentred; beholding a marvellous beauty; then, more than ever, assured of community with the loftiest order; enacting the noblest life, acquiring identity with the divine.*

And his studies and practice have given him the profoundest comprehension of the relations among the *hypostases*. From the One, he says, emanates everything else, but first of all Intellect – the realm of the Forms of all things, both universal and individual.

> *Intellect stands as the image of the One, firstly because there is a certain necessity that the first should have its offspring, carrying onward much of its quality: in other words that there be something in its likeness as the sun's rays tell of the sun.*

And Plotinus speaks of the dependence of the spatio-temporal world on Intellect – that is, of the everyday world we inhabit on the Platonic Forms – the former transient, the latter eternal.

> *The loveliness that is in the sense-realm is an index of the nobleness of the Intellectual sphere, displaying its power and its goodness alike. And all things are forever linked: the one order Intellectual in its being, the other of sense; one self-existent, the other eternally taking its being by participation in that first.*

In like manner he tells us of the realm of Soul – the author of all living things, including the sun, moon, and stars – explaining through the written word the twofold nature of the World-Soul and of all individual souls.

> The World-Soul, as an entirety, governs the universe effortlessly through that part of it which leans to the body side, its lowest part, proceeding by purely intellectual action as in the execution of an artistic conception.
>
> The World-Soul is both one and many: it generates – and, as the life principle, contains – all souls. The individual souls are preoccupied by sensation, and thus they take in much that clashes with their nature and brings distress and trouble, since the very object of their concern is partial, deficient, exposed to many alien influences, filled with desires of its own: pleasure is its lure.
>
> But there is always the other, the transcendent part of soul – that which finds no savour in passing pleasure, but looks to something greater.

Thus from the One men come to be, souls embodied in form, separate yet part of the One at the centre, living in the lowest realm, that of matter, but fully capable of turning away from the base toward the Highest and, like Plotinus himself, becoming one with It.

At this very moment Plotinus is contemplating a treatise he recently wrote. He does not reread his works in order to correct errors, for his eyesight is even worse than it was last year. But his written words are his constant company and he remembers them well. In fact, so firmly stored in his mind is his philosophy that he is able to write everything down, without the least hesitation, in one sitting – even on the occasions when he is obliged to converse with visitors during his writing. Closing his eyes, he performs a familiar exercise of the spirit as he recalls to mind the words almost exactly as they flowed from his pen. He begins to recite the text from memory.

> Our subject is the arche, or principle, of all – that which is The Good and which is Prior to everything; therefore we must strike for those Firsts,

rising away from things of sense-perception, which are the lasts. And we shall ask: What is the One? Where is the pathway to the One? and What is the mystical experience of the One?

First, we must ascend to the Principle within ourselves; from many, we must become one. Only so do we attain to knowledge of that which is Principle and Unity. It is through Nous, or Intellect, that we have this vision of The Unity. It must be our care to bring over nothing whatever from sense-perception, to allow nothing even of soul to enter into the Intellectual realm: with Intellect pure, and with the summit of Intellect, we are to see the All-Pure.

If the quester has the impression of extension or shape or mass attaching to That Nature he has not been led by Intellect, which is not of the order to see such things. The activity has been of sense-perception and of the judgement following upon sense. But only Intellect can inform us of the things of its scope: in particular, its Prior, that Ultimate which came before It — and therefore before Soul — and which is purer than it.

The Unity, then, is not Intellect but something higher still. Intellect is still a being, but that First is no being but rather precedes all Being: it cannot be a being for a being has what we may call the shape of its reality, but The Unity is without shape, even Intellectual shape.

Generative of all, The Unity is none of all; neither thing nor quantity nor quality nor intellect nor soul; not in motion, not at rest, not in place, not in time. It is the self-defined, unique in form or, better, formless, existing before Form was, or Movement or Rest, all of which are attachments of Being and make Being the diversity that it is.

But how, if The Unity is not in movement, can it be other than at rest?

The answer is that movement and rest are states pertaining to Being, and the One precedes all Being. Besides, anything at rest is not simple, for it is something and it is at rest. The One, on the other hand, is simple and therefore we cannot attribute a quality to it.

Now, awareness of this Principle comes neither by knowing nor by the Intellection that discovers the Intellectual Beings — such as the Platonic Forms — but by a presence overpassing all knowledge. In knowing, soul or mind abandons its unity; it cannot remain simple. Knowing is taking account of things; that accounting is multiple; the mind thus plunging into number and multiplicity departs from unity.

Our way then takes us beyond knowing. There may be no wandering from unity; knowing and knowable must all be left aside. Every object of thought, even the highest, we must pass by, for all that is good is later than This and derives from This as from the sun derives all the light of the day.

"Not to be told; not to be written": in our writing and telling we are but urging towards it. To those desiring to see, we point the path. Our teaching is of the road and the travelling; the seeing must be the very act of one that has made this choice.

There are those that have not attained to see. The soul has not come to know the splendour There. Or struck perhaps by that authentic light, all the soul lit by the nearness gained, we have gone weighted from beneath. The vision is frustrated; we still cling to that which keeps us back. We are not yet made over into unity.

From none is that Principle absent and yet from all: present, it remains absent except to those fit to receive, who have prepared themselves and are able to touch it closely by their likeness to it and by a kindred power within themselves through which, remaining as it was when it came to them from the Supreme, they are enabled to see, in so far as God may at all be seen.

In order to see, one must accept that there is another nature than body, and have some conception of it. We are speaking of the One from which emanate, first, the realm of Intellect, and then, from this latter, Soul – both the World-Soul and the individual souls of men, animals, and plants – as well as that baser, formless possibility of form we call "matter": that One which has many other names – Unity, First, Prior, Ultimate, The Good, Supreme – all of which point to, though never encompass, It.

That awesome Prior, The Unity, eludes our knowledge. We must approach it through its offspring, Being. We know it as cause of existence to Intellect, as fount of all that is best, as that which, everlasting and undiminishing, generates all beings and is not to be counted among these, its derivatives, to all of which it must be prior. We can name it only The Unity, understanding that it is not the unity of some other thing. And we strive at the same time to bring our own minds to unity.

In what sense, then, do we assert this Unity and how are we to conceive it?

Use your understanding to imagine this Unity as beyond the most perfect unity you can imagine, not infinite as in measureless extension or quantity but in fathomless depths of power. For This is utterly a self-existent, with no concomitant whatever. This self-sufficing is the essence of its unity. There must be something supremely adequate, autonomous, all-transcending, most utterly without need.

In the Solitary there is neither knowing nor anything unknown. Unity, self-present, has no need of self-intellection: indeed this "self-presence" were better left out, the more surely to preserve the unity. We must eliminate all knowing and all association, all intellection whether internal or external.

This Principle is not, therefore, to be identified with the good of which it is the source; it is good in the unique mode of being The Good above all that is good.

Thus, we must withdraw completely from the external and direct ourselves wholly inwards: no leaning to the outer, the totality of things ignored, the self put out of mind in the contemplation of the Supreme. For the One, while containing no otherness, is ever present with us; we are present with it when we put otherness away. It is not that the Supreme reaches out to us seeking our communion: we reach towards the Supreme; it is we that become present. We are ever before the Supreme – to be cut off is utter dissolution. When we look, we reach Him.

Thus the soul looks upon the wellspring of Life, wellspring also of Intellect, beginning of Being, fount of Good, root of Soul. It is not that these are poured out from the Supreme, lessening it as if it were a thing of mass. In that case the emanants would be perishable. But they are eternal; they spring from an eternal principle, which produces them not by its fragmentation but in virtue of its intact identity. Therefore they too hold firm; so long as the sun shines, so long there will be light.

Our being is the fuller for our turning toward the Good. To hold aloof is loneliness and lessening. Here is the soul's peace, outside of evil; here its true knowing; here it is immune. Here is living, the true, whereas all living apart from Him is but a shadow, a mimicry. Life in the Supreme is the native activity of Intellect; in virtue of that converse it brings forth

*gods, beauty, righteousness, all moral good. For with all these the soul
is pregnant when it has been filled with God. This state is its first and its
final, because from God it comes, its good lies There, and, once turned
to God again, it is what it was. Life here, with the things of earth, is a
sinking, a defeat, a failing of the wing.*

*The soul in its nature loves God and longs to be at one with Him in
the noble love of a daughter for a noble father; but coming to human
birth and lured by the courtships of this sphere, she takes up with another
love, a mortal one, leaves her father and falls.*

*But one day coming to hate her shame, she puts away the evil of
earth, once more seeks the father, and finds her peace.*

*Those to whom all this experience is strange may understand by way
of our earthly longings and the joy we have in gaining that which we
most desire — remembering always that here what we love is perishable,
hurtful, that our loving is of mimicries and turns awry because all was
a mistake, our good was not here, this was not what we sought. Only
There resides our true love and There we may hold it and be with it,
possess it in its verity no longer submerged in alien flesh.*

*Any that have seen know what I have in mind: the soul takes another
life as it approaches God. Thus restored it feels that the dispenser of
true life is There to see, that now we have nothing to look for but, far
otherwise, that we must put aside all else and rest in This alone, This
become, all the earthly environment done away, so that with our being
entire we may cling about This, no part in us remaining, for through it
we have touch with God.*

*And in that touch there are not two; beholder is one with beheld. The
man formed by this mingling with the Supreme must carry its image
impressed upon him. He is become the Unity; no movement now, no
passion, no outlooking desire, once this ascent is achieved; reasoning
is in abeyance and all Intellection and even, to dare the word, the very
self. Caught away, filled with God, he has in perfect stillness attained
isolation; all the being calmed, he turns neither to this side nor to that,
not even inwards to himself. Utterly resting he has become very rest. He
belongs no longer to the order of the beautiful; he has risen beyond beauty.
He has overpassed even the choir of the virtues. He is like one who, having
penetrated the inner sanctuary, leaves the temple images behind him.*

Thus a man outgrows Being, becomes identical with the Transcendent of Being. The self thus lifted, we are in the likeness of the Supreme: we have reached the Limit of all our journeying. Fallen back again, we waken the virtue within until we know ourselves all order once more. Once more we are lightened of the burden and move by virtue towards Intellect and through the Wisdom in That to the Supreme.

This is the life of gods and of the godlike and blessed among men, liberation from the alien that besets us here, a life taking no pleasure in the things of earth, the passing of solitary to solitary.

These are the words of Plotinus, spoken reverently in contemplative mood. As the greatest Empire the world has known sinks inexorably toward collapse, the philosopher, utterly independent of such trifles, rises toward the limit of the soul's ascent, ever eager to exchange terrestrial despair for the sweet light of transcendent Truth. His attention directed inward to his own centre, he seeks and finds the ultimate unity with that greater Centre at the core of the world: the ineffable One.

EPILOGUE

To be a philosopher is not merely to have subtle thoughts, nor even
to found a school, but so to love wisdom as to live according to its
dictates, a life of simplicity, independence, magnanimity, and trust.

THOREAU

We have seen the philosophers of the ancient world, their lives
and their words. They looked to the stars: divinities, symbols of
all the mysteries which men would know, burning rocks in the
heavens. They gazed in wonder, shunning such trifles as wealth
and honour and power, happily relinquishing hereditary titles and
offices.

They sought to explain the eternal flux, the nature of Being,
the ultimate Reality behind the apparent world of sense: the *arche*,
or principle, of the world.

They extolled the contemplative life, the tranquil life, the
simple life, the self-sufficient life, the unseen life away from the
trappings of the multitude.

They questioned themselves and others, striving to improve
both.

They invented logic and scientific thought and conducted
research into the nature of things, subjecting all to rational inquiry,
uniting theory and practice, discourse and action, in the way of
life known as *philosophia*.

They denounced false piety, discovering in their ponderings

the blessed and perfect nature of gods, finding that true piety consists in partaking of divinity, in imitation; they did not make men of gods, but rather strove to make gods of men.

They healed, their philosophy a perennial *therapeia* of spiritual exercises for the soul burdened with the sickness of human society – exercises which transformed and guided the individual toward that perfection of spirit whose hallmarks are virtue and serenity.

They faced an indifferent, even hostile, world; estranged from the manifold folly of everyday secular and religious life, they remained ready always to sacrifice for their chosen way of being.

They sought to understand death, to meditate upon it, to accept it, to overcome it.

They invented Idealism in the world of Forms beyond the world of sense, and Materialism in the world of atoms and void; their vision was accordingly mystical or practical, conservative or progressive, reactionary or radical.

They craved, in a harsh world, the security which nourishes the tranquil soul, and they found it through justice and friendship.

Thrown, unbidden, into conscious existence, as are all mortals, they ceaselessly asked: *What is the good life, and how is it to be achieved?* They found the answer in *eudaimonia* – happiness, or flourishing; they found the pathway, variously, in virtue, pleasure, contemplation, silence, simplicity, mystical union. Along with their chosen life went Reason, hand in hand, questioning, choosing, justifying, questioning again. This was the love of wisdom as it existed in the ancient world. This was philosophy.

Now they are gone. The world waits almost a century for the arrival of Augustine: Bishop of Hippo, Saint from North Africa, the first great Christian philosopher. Less than a century after Augustine's death, the emperor Justinian will formally put an end to Graeco-Roman philosophy when in AD 529, by edict, he closes the Athenian Academy. Philosophy thereafter plays handmaiden to theology for almost a thousand years. Yet the partnership of philosophy and science is by no means at an end. The rational-practical dimension of philosophy will come to life again in that age known as the Renaissance, and then to full flower in the modern era, moderated always by the conflict between Idealism and Materialism. But that is another story.

Meanwhile, our encounter leaves us with a question that begs a response: *What is the good life, and how is it to be achieved?* In an age of decline, it is obligatory to ask also: *What is the role of philosophy in bringing about those individual and social transformations which are indispensable to the flourishing of humankind, or, more fundamentally, of the Earth and all that dwells upon it?* The realm of humanity is not yet filled with that *eudaimonia*, or happiness, of which the ancients so often spoke – and which means literally "a good god within." Thus, we need not ask of what use is philosophy, for we have seen that it is not only a means of understanding, and a way of being, but also an invitation to perfect the human world. The pathway is there for *us* to follow, trodden already by those forerunners whose footsteps yet remain: *the stargazers*.

CHRONOLOGY

A boldface entry indicates the subject of a chapter in this book.

BC

1500   o *Vedas* (c. 1500-c. 900)

1400   o **Marduk reigns as supreme god of Babylon**
       o ***Enuma elish* ("When above") recited at Babylonian New Year Festival**

1300   o Trojan War; Greeks sack Troy (c. 1220)

1200   o Mycenaean civilization ends; literacy disappears
       o Palaces destroyed throughout southern Greece
       o Dark Age (1150-800): migration of mainland Greeks to Asia Minor
       o Age of Hebrew prophets (c. 900-c. 600)

800   o Rise of Greek *polis* (city-state)
       o Greek colonization of southern Italy, Sicily, Asia Minor, and the Black Sea
       o Rise of aristocracies throughout Greece
       o Introduction of the Phoenecian alphabet in Greece
       o First Olympic Games (776)
       o *Upanishads* (c. 800-c. 300)
       o Founding of Rome (753)
       o Homer: *Iliad, Odyssey*

- Hesiod: *Theogony, Works and Days*
- Greek art, literature, and architecture begin to flourish

700
- Coinage introduced from Lydia to Greece
- Bustling Miletus becomes the birthplace of philosophy
- Zoroaster
- Solon
- Sappho

600
- Greeks establish Massalia (Marseilles) and trade with Celts
- **Thales, Anaximander, Anaximenes**: first philosophers of the western world
- Pisistratus, tyrant of Athens
- King Croesus of Lydia conquers Ionia (but not Miletus)
- Temple of Artemis at Ephesus
- **Pythagoras of Samos**
- **Xenophanes of Colophon**
- Cleisthenes introduces Athenian democracy
- Lao-Tse: *Tao Te Ching*
- Buddha
- Confucius: *Analects*
- **Heraclitus of Ephesus**
- Temple of Apollo at Delphi

500
- **Parmenides** of Elea
- Persian Wars: Marathon (490), Salamis (480)
- Aeschylus: *Oresteia*
- Greek literature: Pindar, Hecataeus, Simonides, Bacchylides
- **Zeno** of Elea
- Delian League founded by Athens; later becomes Athenian empire
- Apex of Athenian democracy; height of Spartan and Corinthian power
- Pericles leads Athens (461-429)
- **Aspasia**, courtesan and philosopher
- Pheidias, sculptor

- Temple-building on the Acropolis (Parthenon, 438 BC)
- Empedocles of Acragas
- **Anaxagoras of Clazomenae**
- Plague at Athens (429); death of Pericles
- Hippocrates, physician
- Sophocles: *Oedipus the King*
- **Protagoras** the Sophist
- Herodotus: *Histories*
- Peloponnesian War (431-404): Athens defeated by Sparta
- Hippocrates and early medicine
- **Socrates**
- **Democritus of Abdera**: atomistic materialism
- Euripides: *Bacchae*
- Aristophanes: *Clouds*
- Thucydides: *History of the Peloponnesian War*

400
- Spartan domination of Greece
- Xenophon, historian: *Anabasis, Hellenica*
- **Plato**: *Republic;* the Academy
- Theatre at Epidauros
- **Diogenes of Sinope**: the Cynic
- **Aristotle**: *Metaphysics, Nichomachean Ethics;* the Lyceum
- Theban domination of Greece
- Philip of Macedon rules Greece (338)
- **Pyrrho of Elis**: Scepticism
- Alexander the Great builds an empire (336-323)
- Hellenistic Age begins (323) with death of Alexander
- Theophrastus, Aristotle's successor at the Lyceum
- Decline of Greek *polis*
- Hellenistic kingdoms of Egypt, Greece, and Asia Minor
- Menander's comedies
- **Epicurus** and the Garden
- Zeno of Citium founds Stoicism
- Rise of Roman power in Mediterranean
- Aristarchus: heliocentric theory
- Euclid's geometry: *Elements*

300   o Arcesilaus founds the Middle Academy
      o Cleanthes, Chrysippus: successive heads of Stoic
        school
      o Archimedes – mathematician, astronomer, inventor:
        "Eureka!"
      o Eratosthenes measures Earth's circumference
      o Hannibal defeated by Romans at Zama (202)

200   o Plautus, Terence: Roman comic theatre
      o Carneades and New Academy: scepticism
      o Roman sack of Corinth (146) ends Greek
        independence
      o Greece becomes a Roman province
      o Panaetius becomes head of Stoic school

100   o Spartacus slave revolt crushed (71)
      o Cicero
      o Posidonius continues Stoicism
      o Lucretius' Epicurean poem: *De rerum natura* (*On the Nature
        of Things*)
      o Julius Caesar
      o End of Roman republic; Augustus becomes emperor
      o End of Hellenistic Period
      o Augustan (Golden) Age of Roman Literature: Virgil,
        Livy, Horace, Ovid

AD   o Jesus Christ
      o Seneca: Roman Stoicism
      o St. Paul in Greece
      o Pliny the Elder: *Naturalis Historia*
      o Destruction of Pompei by Vesuvius eruption (79)
      o Silver Age of Roman Literature:
      o Tacitus, Suetonius, Pliny the Younger, Martial, Juvenal,
        Quintilian
      o Rise of Christianity and Church

100   o Gradual development and refinement of Roman legal
        system

- Plutarch: *Parallel Lives*
- Danubian wars begin
- Roman Empire reaches its greatest extent under Trajan (98-117)
- **Epictetus** the Stoic: philosopher-slave
- Ptolemy: astronomy, trigonometry
- Hadrian's Wall, Roman Pantheon
- Galen writes on medicine
- **Marcus Aurelius**: philosopher-king

200
- Diogenes Laertius: *Lives of Eminent Philosophers*
- Sextus Empiricus: *Outlines of Pyrrhonism*
- **Plotinus**, Neoplatonist: *Enneads*
- Porphyry, disciple of Plotinus
- Invasions of the Roman Empire from the north-east

300
- Constantinople becomes seat of Roman Empire (331)
- Roman Empire divided into east and west after death of Theodosius (395)

400
- Saint Augustine: *Confessions, City of God*
- Western Roman Empire falls to Germans under Odoacer (476)

500
- Boethius: *Consolation of Philosophy*
- Emperor Justinian closes the schools of philosophy (529)

600

NOTES

Public Domain Translations

Material from the following public domain translations appears in altered form, woven into the text at various points:

Hicks, R.D. (trans.). *Diogenes Laertius. Lives of Eminent Philosophers*. Cambridge, MA: Loeb, 1925.

Jowett, B. (trans.). *Plato. The Dialogues of Plato*. New York: Charles Scribner, 1871.

King, L.W. (trans.). *The Seven Tablets of Creation*. London: Luzac and Co., 1902.

Long, George (trans.). *Epictetus. Enchiridion*. Mineola: Dover, 2004.

Long, George (trans.). *Marcus Aurelius. Meditations*. Mineola: Dover, 1997.

Mackenna, Stephen (trans.). *Plotinus. The Enneads*. Harmondsworth: Penguin, 1991.

Ross, W.D. (trans.). *Aristotle. Nichomachean Ethics*. Oxford: Clarendon Press, 1908.

Yonge, C.D. (trans.). *Diogenes Laertius. The Lives and Opinions of Eminent Philosophers*. 2nd Edition. London: George Bell & Sons, 1895.

Collections of the Fragments

Presocratic fragments appearing in the text are paraphrasings from comparisons of the following sources of fragments of the works of the philosophers:

Barnes, Jonathan. *Early Greek Philosophy*. Harmondsworth: Penguin, 1987.

Hicks, R.D. (trans.). *Diogenes Laertius. Lives of Eminent Philosophers.* Cambridge, MA: Loeb, 1925.

Inwood, B. and Gerson, L.P. *Hellenistic Philosophy: Introductory Readings.* Indianapolis: Hackett, 1998.

Kirk, G.S., Raven, J.E., and Schofield, M. *The Presocratic Philosophers.* Second Edition. Cambridge: Cambridge University Press, 1983. (This work contains both the original Greek fragments and their translation.)

Robinson, John Mansley. *An Introduction to Early Greek Philosophy.* Boston: Houghton Mifflin Co., 1968.

Yonge, C.D. (trans.). *Diogenes Laertius. The Lives and Opinions of Eminent Philosophers.* 2nd Edition. London: George Bell & Sons, 1895.

CHAPTER NOTES

Prologue

Information on women philosophers of the ancient world can be found in Gilles Ménage's *The History of Women Philosophers*, trans. Beatrice H. Zedler (Boston: University of America, 1985). The notion that ancient philosophy was first and foremost a way of life, secondarily a discourse, has been convincingly argued for by the French scholar Pierre Hadot in, among other works, his excellent *What Is Ancient Philosophy?*, trans. Michael Chase (Cambridge, MA and London: Harvard University Press, 2004).

Chapter I

The version of the *Enuma elish* which appears in part in this chapter is adapted from L.W. King's public domain translation, *The Seven Tablets of Creation* (London: Luzac and Co., 1902). Other classic works containing background material are the following: Frankfort, Henri et al., *Before Philosophy* (Chicago: University of Chicago Press, 1946); Frankfort, H., *Kingship and the Gods* (Chicago: University of Chicago Press, 1948); Langdon, S., *The Babylonian Epic of Creation* (Oxford: Clarendon, 1923); and Thomson, G., *Studies in Ancient Greek Society: The First Philosophers*, 2nd Edition (London: Lawrence & Wishart, 1961).

Chapter II
The portrait of Miletus, the birthplace of western philosophy and science, is based on the excellent description given in Auguste Jardé's classic, *The Formation of the Greek People*, trans. M.R. Dobie (New York: Cooper Square Publishers, 1971).

Chapter IV
Since Pythagoras wrote nothing, it has always been difficult for scholars to separate his contributions to Pythagoreanism from those of later members of the school. Walter Burkert's *Lore and Science in Ancient Pythagoreanism*, trans. E.L. Minar, Jr. HUP: Cambridge, MA, 1972, a classic (and difficult) work of scholarship, tackles this problem while challenging many traditional ideas concerning Pythagoras and the early Pythagoreans. More recent studies include *Pythagoras and the Pythagoreans: A Brief History*, Indianapolis: Hackett, 2001 and Christoph Riedweg's *Pythagoras: His Life, Teaching and Influence*, trans. Steven Rendall, Ithaca: Cornell, 2005.

Chapter VII–IX
For a readable account of the mystical significance of Parmenides' and Empedocles' poems, and a complete re-evaluation of Eleatic philosophy, see Peter Kingsley's *In Search of the Dark Places of Wisdom* (Inverness, CA: Golden Sufi Center, 1999) as well as its sequel, *Reality* (Inverness, CA: Golden Sufi Center, 2003).

Chapter XIII
The story of Socrates' trial in this chapter is based on Jowett's public domain translation of Plato's *Apology*.

Chapter XV
The account of Plato's lecture at the Academy is based on Jowett's public domain translation of *The Republic*.

Chapter XVII
Aristotle's lecture at the Lyceum is based on the W.D. Ross public domain translation of *Nichomachean Ethics*.

Chapter XX

The entries in Marcus Aurelius' journal are based on George Long's public domain translation of the *Meditations;* quotations of Epictetus, on Long's public domain translation of the *Enchiridion,* or *Manual.*

Chapter XXI

The writings of Plotinus found in this chapter are a modified version of those contained in the public domain text of Stephen Mackenna's masterful translation of *The Enneads.*

FURTHER READING

General Works

Ackrill, J.L. (ed.). *Aristotle. A New Aristotle Reader.* Princeton: Princeton University Press, 1988. A nice selection of material from the writings of "the Master of those who know."

Barnes, J. *Early Greek Philosophy.* Harmondsworth· Penguin, 1987. An excellent collection, with commentary, of the fragments of the Presocratic philosophers.

Hadot, P. *What Is Ancient Philosophy?* Trans. M. Chase. Cambridge, MA and London: Harvard University Press, 2004. An excellent introduction to the notion of philosophy as "a way of life," beautifully written and translated.

Hussey, E. *The Presocratics.* Indianapolis: Hackett, 1972. A standard undergraduate text on the early Greek philosophers.

Inwood, B. and Gerson, L.P. *Hellenistic Philosophy: Introductory Readings.* Indianapolis: Hackett, 1998. A good source of the writings of the Sceptics, Epicureans, and Stoics.

Sharples, R.W. *Stoics, Epicureans and Sceptics: An introduction to Hellenistic Philosophy.* London; New York: Routledge, 1996. A standard undergraduate text giving a good overview.

Staniforth, M. (trans.). *Marcus Aurelius. Meditations.* Harmondsworth: Penguin, 1964. An affordable and enjoyable translation of Marcus' thoughts.

Tredennick, H. and Tarrant, H. (trans). *Plato. The Last Days of Socrates: Euthyphro/Apology/Crito/Phaedo.* Harmondsworth: Penguin, 1995.

186 STARGAZERS

Good dialogues with which to begin to sense Plato's style and Socrates' character. Other editions will also suffice.

Histories of Philosophy

Bogomolov, A.S. *History of Ancient Philosophy*. Trans. V. Stankevich. Moscow: Progress, 1985. A thorough history, written from a materialist perspective, including a considerable amount of social and historical background to ancient philosophy. Unfortunately, the book lacks an index.

Copleston, Frederick. *A History of Philosophy*. Vol. 1, Garden City: Doubleday, 1962. A respected history of philosophy by a Catholic scholar.

Gaarder, Jostein. *Sophie's World*. Trans. Paulette Møller. New York: Farrar, Straus and Giroux, 1994. This best-seller is, as its subtitle states, "a novel about the history of philosophy."

Marías, Julian. *History of Philosophy*. Trans. S. Appelbaum and C. C. Stowbridge. New York: Dover, 1967. A very readable history which includes many minor philosophers as well as all the major ones up to the middle of the twentieth century.

Russell, Bertrand. *A History of Western Philosophy*. London: George Allen & Unwin, 1961. The most famous history of western philosophy "in its connection with social and political circumstances." Delightful reading from a humanist and master of clarity.

Reference Works

Honderich, Ted. *The Oxford Companion to Philosophy*. Oxford; New York: Oxford University Press, 1995. A very comprehensive dictionary of western philosophy.

Reese, William L. *Dictionary of Philosophy and Religion: Eastern and Western Thought*. Expanded Edition. Amherst: Humanity Books, 1999. Another excellent dictionary of philosophy with many unique features, including chronological treatments of major philosophical themes.

O books
O is a symbol of the world, of oneness and unity. In different cultures it also means the "eye", symbolizing knowledge and insight, and in Old English it means "place of love or home". O books explores the many paths of understanding which different traditions have developed down the ages, particularly those today that express respect for the planet and all of life. In philosophy, metaphysics and aesthetics O as zero relates to infinity, indivisibility and fate. In Zero Books we are developing a list of provocative shorter titles that cross different specializations and challenge conventional academic or majority opinion.

For more information on the full list of over 300 titles please visit our website
www.O-books.net

myspiritradio is an exciting web, internet, podcast and mobile phone global broadcast network for all those interested in teaching and learning in the fields of body, mind, spirit and self development. Listeners can

hear the show online via computer or mobile phone, and even download their favourite shows to listen to on MP3 players whilst driving, working, or relaxing.

Feed your mind, change your life with O Books,
The O Books radio programme carries interviews with most authors, sharing their wisdom on life, the universe and everything...e mail questions and co-create the show with O Books and myspiritradio.

Just visit **www.myspiritradio.com** for more information.